Windmill Heroes 2

Introduction

Welcome to Windmill Heroes 2 a celebration of football in Royal Leamington Spa, Warwick and Kenilworth. Since Windmill Heroes was published Leamington Football Club has confirmed that the history of the club has been revised.

After extensive research by club historian Paul Vanes has led to the discovery that there is no connection between the current club and that of Leamington Town. They are in fact two separate entities. The club as we know it today was born, in 1933, as Lockheed, Borg & Beck.

There is a common misconception that Lockheed/AP Leamington are not the same club as Leamington FC because of the twelve year gap in our playing record, which is emphatically not the case.

We have to thank Paul for his hard work researching the history of the club. Leamington Town FC were the pioneers of football in the town and we should always appreciate them. In this book we will have a look at some of the great moments in Leamington Town's history.

Leamington and Warwick has a proud history of amateur and semi-professional football, we are going to have a look at some of the great teams and players which I hope will bring back happy memories for fans.

Our journey will also include Lockheed Leamington, AP Leamington, Leamington FC, Kenilworth and Racing Club Warwick. Memories and anecdotes from former and current players, I hope you enjoy this book.

Chapter One – Westlea Wanderers

If you know football in the town of Royal Leamington Spa then you would have heard of Westlea Wanderers. We are going to go on a journey celebrating this remarkable football team's story from the early days of the mid-1960s to the present day. Westlea Wanderers are now Leamington's most famous Sunday league team, some of the towns greatest players have played for the club and also played for Leamington FC and Racing Club Warwick.

Westlea Wanderers were formed in 1965 by a group of lads living in the Kingsway and Westlea Road area of the town. In the early 1960s a number players who went onto play for Westlea were part of Oken High School's very good team. Oken High School (now called Myton School) won the Mid-Warwickshire Schools Intermediate Cup on 18th March 1961 , this team was never beaten they had some great players.

Oken's team was – Mick Clarkson(Goalkeeper) John Rose, Mick Coop, Ian Walker, Bob Phillips, Pete Summerfield, Tom Denholm, Jimmy Collins , Geoff Iredale, Mick Bolton, Dennis Farr.

Mick Coop went onto play for Coventry City. Ian Walker and Dennis Farr played for Coventry City's youth team and were both founder members of Westlea Wanderers first team in 1965.

John Rose and Tom Denholm played for Racing Club Warwick. Bob Phillips also played for Racing Club and AP Leamington. The name that really stands out is Mick Coop; he was born in Grimsby but grew up in Leamington Spa. Mick went onto have a long successful career in professional football joining Coventry City's youth ranks in 1963 then becoming a legend at Highfield Road making 499 appearances. Most of his career he played at right back but also played in central defence, Mick also played for York City, Detroit Express, Derby County and finishing his career with AP Leamington in the 1983/84 season. Mick Coop played for Milverton Villa in the early 1960s; Geoff Bott told me that he and his brother Reg, Mick and Ian Walker played in a tournament in Rotterdam. This would have been 1961 or 1962 they were still at school. Geoff himself played for Whitnash and recalls Syd Hall (Brakes) played for the other side. The gulf in class was unbelievable "he hammered us on his own"

Mick whilst playing for Coventry City in the 1960s played against another Leamington lad David Woodfield who went to Campion Secondary Modern School. David who lived in Cashmore Avenue signed for Wolverhampton Wanderers aged fifteen in the late 1950s. Wolves and the Sky Blues played each other in the First and Second Divisions, most famously in the 1966/67 season when Coventry pipped Wolves for the title.

Keith Gould

I spoke to Keith on the phone, he was one of the founder members of the first ever Westlea Wanderers team in 1965. Keith told me that Ian Walker was a big Wolves fan and so the team was called Wanderers after his heroes from Molineux. As a young player Keith spent time at Coventry City aged fifteen or sixteen, he didn't really enjoy it. Bobby Gould would have been at Coventry the same time he is no relation.

Keith attended Blackdown High School which is now North Leamington School they had a very good football team. In his playing days he was an inside left/left half, Keith played for Saturday team Avon Rovers teammates included – Tom Denholm, Bob Phillips, Tony Aston, Chris Elliott and John Rose.

Keith's most famous goal is the winner in the Birmingham Junior Cup v Poplar Athletic in 1972. Westlea Wanderers were at their peak then, possibly Leamington's best ever Sunday League team.

Keith talked about the great players at Westlea Wanderers Ian Walker, Ian Montgomery, Sid Bench and Mick Chimes.

Thanks for your time Keith.

Pepe Gill

I spoke to Pep, in his playing days he was a fine right back he played junior football for Leamington Boys Club and North Leamington under 18s. Senior Teams South Leamington on a Saturday and when Sunday League Seniors Started he played for North Leamington. Pep Signed for Westlea Wanderers in 1968 where he was captain at one stage. Unfortunately he suffered a bad knee injury (Cartlidge) and he didn't play in the Junior Cup Final in 1972. Pep trained at Racing Club Warwick with John Rose, Chris Elliott and Malc Hyland who all played for Racing Club on a Saturday and Westlea on Sundays.

Pep also played for AP Works, a season with Whittle Wanderers and back to Westlea he was also part of a very good Leamington Southend team. Pep talked about some of the great players he played with like Ivor Talbot, Keith Jones and Tony Partridge who was an excellent goalkeeper. The best team he played in was the Westlea Wanderers side of the 1970/71 season players like Ian Walker and Barry Whitlock were both legends.

Sadly on 20th December 2019 Pep suddenly passed away, my sincere condolences to his family and friends. I only spoke to Pep once but I could tell that he was a lovely man who will be very much missed by everyone who knew him.

A tribute to Pep by Don Grantham

Pep was a stalwart of the local football scene. He played at the top level of local amateur Saturday and Sunday football as an accomplished full back from his teenage years until his late thirties. He served Winsams and South Leamington as a youngster and AP Works later in his career in the Saturday League. Pep played for Leamington Southend and Westlea Wanderers in the top flight of the Leamington Sunday League, all with great distinction. He was a member of many Championship and Cup Winning teams. After retiring from playing, he worked tirelessly behind the scenes in numerous capacities, and supported Westlea Wanderers tirelessly right through to his sudden and untimely passing. An example of Pep's character and support for local youngsters, and local football was that in recent and this season, giving his time to prepare after match meals for Leamington Hibs and their opponents after their home games at Cubbington Club.

He was a tenacious opponent and competitor, although a very fair man with huge integrity. Pep was a rare; breed; someone who everyone has something good to say about, and about whom no one had a bad word to say! He was a close friend to many. Pep was best man at Ian and Christine Walker's wedding; best man at Ian and Kath Montgomery's wedding.

Pep was a very close friend of mine from the age of fifteen. I made my debut for Westlea Wanderers in which he was a regular. From 1971 until his sad passing on December 19th 2019, 48 years! A remarkable man who touched everyone he met, and will be hugely missed.

Ken Lambert

I contacted Ken via email, he is Chris Walker's brother (Ian's brother in law) Ken during his playing days was a goalkeeper and was Westlea Wanderers secretary in the 1970s.

How did you football career begin and what teams did you play for?

In 1958 I started at Leamington Boys Club, a year later in 1959 I joined North Leamington FC. In 1960 I played for St Marys Leamington, around this time I signed for Whitnash FC as well. I also had a couple of years with Henry Griffiths FC (the jewellery factory in Leamington Spa until they sold their ground off). In 1967 I Moved to Sutton Coldfield and played for the Police team there and occasionally for Warwickshire Police. I moved back to Leamington in 1972 and had a few games with Mid Warwick's Police in the Police League.
In the early seventies signed for Leamington Hibernians on a Saturday and Avana Sports in the Division Three Leamington Sunday League. In the mid-Seventies I signed for Westlea Wanderers FC on a Sunday and AP Work's team on a Saturday (only now and again.)
In 1979 had a back operation and was advised to give up football (I was

always a goalkeeper) and went on to be Westlea's club secretary. I held that role only for a year though as I moved to Coventry in 1980.

For a brief time in the mid-1970s, the Heathcote Pub had a Saturday team and I turned out for them a few times.

Did you play with Ian at Westlea Wanderers?

Yes I played with Ian through the couple of years I had with Westlea. Ian was a great captain and a rock in the back four in front of me. My first real competitive game with a club was, as I mentioned, with Leamington Boys Club. Mick Coop was one of the full backs. Pepe Gill the other. Westlea had too many good players to mention. Ian Montgomery, Sid Bench, Mel Broome, Paul Coleman to name a few.

Thank you very much for sharing your memories Ken.

Gerry Gleeson

Gerry played for Westlea reserves in the 1970s. I asked him a few questions on Facebook.

What teams did you play for?

I played for St Peters Celtic as a youngster then moved to Men's footy with St Dominic's -1970 to 1972, Westlea Wanderers Reserves 1972 to 1975, and Wellesbourne (both Saturday and Sunday sides - forever), Thornbank and Northgate in later years.

What position did you play; you must have played against some great players?

I played up front as a winger or centre forward most of the time, then drifted back to centre midfield and finally ended up playing fullback or sweeper. Certainly did play with or against all the Leamington league greats during the 70s and 80s. I was on the Ford Leamington Plant team that made the final of the Interplant Cup at Rush Green (West Hams Training ground now). The best players from the local Saturday and Sunday leagues at the plant decided to have a go at winning it and we almost did. For two or three seasons we had a real go. We reached the

Semi-finals twice and the final once. Not bad for a Plant with only 500 employees vs the tens of thousands at Halewood, Bridgend and Dagenham

Gerry now lives in Southampton and he often watches the Saints, thank you for your time.

Westlea Wanderers win Birmingham Junior Cup

30th April 1972

Westlea Wanderers finest hour was when they won the Birmingham Sunday Junior Cup beating Poplar Athletic (Bedworth) 1.0 after extra time.

Westlea Wanderers – Dave Garratt, Dave Friend, Syd Bench, Keith Orme, Chris Elliott, Ian Walker, John Rose, Ian Montgomery, Dennis Woodhead, Andy Townsend(Mick Chimes) Keith Gould.

Half backs Orme, Elliott and Walker were superb. Ian Walker was an inspired captain for the Leamington team. Keith Orme had a chance for Westlea on twenty minutes heading over the bar from a Townsend corner. Poplar's main goal threat came from ex Lockheed player Les Sanders and Roger Taylor; it was Taylor who forced a good save from Garratt and a fine tackle from Friend. Westlea's Montgomery saw a shot clip the post, with the score at 0.0 they headed into extra time.

Rose tested the keeper with a scissor kick, but it was Gould who finally broke the deadlock assisted by Chimes. Westlea had further chances but had to settle for the one goal which gave the club their finest hour.

Westlea Wanderers win Cancer Cup

4th May 1974

Westlea won the Leamington Cancer Cup for the first time after beating Wellesbourne A 2.1 after extra time. Dennis Woodhead was the hero scoring two goals. Maynard scored Wellesbourne's goal.

Wellesbourne A –

Myatt, Bagully, Taylor, Kendry, Stevens, Beechey, Coton, Hayward, Watlng, Maynard, Turvey

Westlea Wanderers –
Garratt,Friend,Bench,Orme,Woodhead,Elliott,Rose,Montgomery,Gould,R Townsend, A Townsend

Modern Era

Dave Draper

Dave is very well known in local football as player and a manager. He comes from a fine Leamington footballing family, his dad Bill was a great centre forward for Lockheed Leamington in the 1950s. Bill's Brother George also played and managed in Leamington. I asked Dave a few questions about his memories of Sunday League football.

What are your memories of your dad and uncle with Whittle Wanderers in the 1970s?

I used to go to watch Whittle Wanderers most Sunday mornings. I would sit it my dad's huge Ford Granada. He wanted me to be close by, so he parked as close to the goal as he could. I used to get out if it was a nice day and sit by the goal ...until one day I took one of the many misplaced shots in the face. I remember Noel Edmonds was always on the car radio.

They played up at Newbold Comyn in those days, on the first pitches if I remember correctly. George used to manage them and played when they were short. I remember Johnny Glenn always being there playing, he also used to do painting and decorating at the house. I saw him in Whitnash shops only the other day! He has not changed a bit.

Did you ever play in a same match with your dad? He was still good into his forties.

I recall one game when my Dad was fifty, we played together for Westlea Reserves v Harbury ....he did all of my running lol.

How did you get involved with Westlea Wanderers and how long were you with them?

I was at Cubbington Albion as an eighteen year old I think, and then some mates of mine who played at Westlea asked me to go along. Ian Walker was the manager at the time.

What your favourite memories of your time playing with Westlea Wanderers?

I played up front with Chris Prophet initially and then players such as Cliff Morby , Ajit Braich, Tony Critten , Ian Montgomery , Don Grantham , Dave McMahon , Stu Smith

I was very lucky to have such a great introduction to top level local football. Most of the players were playing semi pro at Racing Club Warwick or Southam United.

Winning the League by beating our title rivals Stockton away back in the 1990s was special. We had a great team then, managed by Keith Billington. I scored two and I felt that was the best feeling after a long hard season. I scored a few cup final winning goals against Long Itchington, but I always scored against them. (You have those teams that you feel good against)

Another big memory was when I was nineteen when I was playing my Saturday football for V.S Rugby. We were playing Wycombe Wanderers away in the Fourth Qualifying round of the FA Cup. I was lucky enough to score a Hat-trick in a shock 5-1 win.

The next morning I turned up at Pepe's cafe as usual to play for my Sunday team Westlea .Monty said "what are you doing here? I just said we've got Long Itchington today we have got to beat them, he just smiled. I wasn't trying to impress anyone; I just wanted to play for Westlea.

I also phoned in sick to the Worcester City manager on a Tuesday night as I wanted to play against Khalsa in a cup semi-final.....and we lost when Chris Prophet missed a penalty!

One strange moment came when I was managing Westlea Wanderers; we were playing one of the Coventry teams down at the very bottom pitch at Newbold Comyn. A visiting player, off the ball, seriously assaulted one of my players. I stood there and thought this is not right; there was no need for it. The player was eventually sent off after a long commotion.....I still couldn't get my head around what effect that will have on my player - at work, facially or even psychologically. So I got my phone out and called the police, it was only still the first half so I knew they had time to arrive before the end of the game.

Twenty minutes later I saw two police officers walking across the pitches to ours. Then as soon as the aggressor saw them he jumped up and headed over the golf course. The crazy thing was that his colleague, who had done nothing wrong in the game ....also, ran off over the golf course, he may have had something to hide me thinks. Anyway, the officers raised a smile and just radioed their colleagues to intercept them at the gate which they did. The arrest was made and a caution given at a later court case. However I felt my actions were necessary.

It must have been amazing to be part of a club with such great tradition in Leamington?

We won the title and many cups over the years, then in the 1990's I took over as Player Manager. We left the Leamington League for three or four years and joined the Coventry League. Basically Westlea and the Hodcarrier were the only two teams in the Leamington Premier league that could enjoy a good battle, but that left six months of games that were quite predictable.

The Coventry League was an adventure, some of my Westlea colleagues were not so sure ....but no regrets. I left the post after five years and the younger generation returned he team to the Leam league and have been super successful ever since ...which is great. The fifty years celebration of Westlea Wanderers in 2015 was very special.

Thanks for sharing your memories Dave, more from you later in the book about your time with Racing Club Warwick.

Dave Sharpe

Dave is well known now as a Master of Ceremonies, Conference Facilitator, Awards Host, BBC Radio Presenter. In the 1990s he was a coach at Westlea Wanderers I contacted him via email and asked him a few questions.

Did you play much football yourself?

I played for a few Saturday and Sunday sides but mainly in Nuneaton which were Fife Street and Drayton on a Sunday and Shilton on a Saturday. I played at left back a lot but also up front on the left, I'm very left footed! I could take a great corner kick (I've scored a few left foot in swingers!)

How did you get involved with Westlea?

When I moved to Leamington in 1988 I played for Hibs on Saturday and then by chance I met Drapes. He got me in at Westlea and I played in the Reserves in Division One. I was then asked to become reserve team manager because I'd had some experience and I'm also a qualified FA Coach.

Which players stood out during your time with Westlea?

We had a very good team! I think we won the league in my first year but couldn't go up because the first team were already in the Premier Division. I remember Dave Moreton being excellent in goal, Billo on the wing too. Ajit Braich was always impressive. Occasionally a first teamer would play for us like Daz Timms or Dave Ward who were excellent. I had some brilliant times at Westlea, I always remember scoring a hat trick and getting a big ovation when we all met back at the pub. Brilliant lads and people involved like Treddy and Billo. Tommo (a great player) and Drapes of course, when he could be bothered lol. He was such a handful on the pitch.

You and Dave Draper had your own non-league show on radio that must have been enjoyable? Dave is a great guy

Doing the radio show with him was fantastic; I was his guest and then became his sidekick. Eventually I took over the show when he left. We had some heated debates on air too! I'm a Nuneaton fan and he was always supporting Leamington.

Great to hear from you Dave, I enjoyed listening to your radio show back in the day. Thank you for your time.

Ian Billington

I contacted Ian via email and asked him a few questions about his time in football.

How did your career begin and what junior teams did you play for?

My career began at the age of eight when I was asked to go and train with Leamington Hibs under 10s managed by Shaun McFarlane. The following year I stayed with Leamington Hibs in my own age group where I remained the whole of my junior career until aged sixteen. I was mainly managed by Jim Barry who had a massive influence in my footballing career. We were a very successful junior team winning the Mid-Warwickshire boys league four times before moving on to Coventry and Birmingham League for my final two seasons. In this time I also represented Mid-Warwickshire and Warwickshire at school level.

You come from a good footballing family, could you tell me a little about your dad and your son's career?

My dad Keith Billington was a great footballer from a very young age leading him to have trials for Stoke City as a teenager. He played for numerous teams as an adult both Saturdays and Sundays with Leamington South, Westlea Wanderers and AP Works among some of the teams he spent his most time playing for.

My son, Ryan Billington is the footballing son who started his career at the age of seven with Leamington Hibs. He remained there for three years before moving on to join Khalsa where he stayed for the rest of his junior career. During which time he had trials for Leicester City and Coventry City the latter where he played for a year. His Saturday career started at Whitnash Town playing in numerous finals at the Ricoh Arena before moving on to Racing Club Warwick the team where he is currently playing for. It is by no surprise that since the age of fifteen he has been in the Westlea First Team winning the league on every occasion and a number of cups.

What are your memories of the very good Westlea Wanderers team of 1999/2000?

The 1999/2000 season had a very good Westlea team due to the fact we had moved to the Coventry League four years previously and worked our way to the top division. The team consisted of a lot of players who had been with Westlea a long time i.e.: Daz Timms, Simon Walker & Ashley Walker etc. But also had the addition of other top Leamington players for example -Harj Dhesi, Paul Eden, Neil Thompson and numerous others. We held our own and finished second in a very competitive Sunday League all under the guidance of Dave Draper.

Being part of the reformed Leamington team in 2000 must have been amazing, have you got a favourite match?

There were some remarkable moments in the early reformed years of Leamington FC especially the coach trips to away games with all the supporters. I think it goes without saying the first game back at the New

Windmill was just amazing and a highlight in my career. My one memory was going into the changing rooms (shed) after the warm up at around 2:45pm with a crowd of about 150 to then be told by the referee that the game was being put back due to Harbury Lane being gridlocked with cars trying to get into the ground. So when we finally came out to see over 800 fans! The feeling was overwhelming. The game passed so quickly but I do remember having a hand in Josh Blake's first goal.

What other teams have you played for?

Sundays, well this is easy from 1987 (aged fifteen) until present I have been at Westlea where I have also been the manager for the past fifteen years.

Saturdays, like a lot of people I played for many clubs my first club was Pottertons before moving to Racing Club Warwick where I had a couple of spells. I also played for Wellesbourne and Whitnash with the two main clubs being Daventry in the UCL and Leamington in the Midland Combination.

Thank you very much for sharing your memories Ian, you are very much part of Leamington's proud football history.

Westlea Wanderers Coventry Sunday League Division 1 Winners 1999/2000

When Leamington FC reformed in 2000 a core of the squad was part of Westlea Wanderers successful 99/00 season which would have helped create a solid foundation for Leamington's first season after reforming. A few other players in The Brake's early seasons also played for Westlea at some point in their career, Glenn Webb, Guy Rippon and Will Payne.

Westlea Wanderers - Martyn Beeston, Adam Cooper, Paul Frost, Ashley Proctor, Dave Treadwell, Ashley Walker, Simon Walker, Craig Dutton,

Craig Lee, Simon Timms, Billy Hegarty, Dave Draper, Brian Agar, Kevin Ariss, Gavin Hampton, Darren Timms, Adrian Duff, Liam McGovern, Ian Billington

Out of this list of players Kevin Ariss, Liam McGovern and Ian Billington played in Leamington's first game against Enville Athletic on the 19th August 2000.

Dave Draper is part of a small club of players to play for Leamington FC before 1988 and after 2000.

Jamie Coleman

Jamie Like his dad Paul Played for Leamington, A defender Jamie came through the Brakes youth team and made his debut in 2005. I asked Jamie a couple of questions.

Which was the best Westlea team you played in?

The best Westlea side I have played in was the one that won the Birmingham Vase the second season I was there. The following year we were beaten finalists in the Birmingham Senior Cup. The side was Paul O'Keefe Andy McKinley, Lee Scott, Simon Walker, Craig Watkin, Luke Cole, Josh Cole, Glenn Webb, Neil Stacey, Tom Friend, and Jamie Coleman.

Who would you say was the best player that you played with at Westlea?

Brian Agar although coming to the end of his career is the best player I've played with at Westlea. Brilliant player!

Thanks Jamie that was indeed a very good team with players who also played for Leamington FC and Racing Club Warwick.

Nick McFarlane

I contacted Nick via email and Facebook; I worked briefly with Nick in 1997 so it was great to catch up with him.

Could I firstly ask you how you got into football, what junior teams did you play for?

I liked it at school and remember my dad taking me along to the local club; I tried it and loved it. My first club was St. Peter's Celtic for about a year, then St. Josephs Juniors (Whitnash but in the South Birmingham League) for about two or three years. I went back to St. Peters Celtic for two years then Central Ajax when I was fifteen/sixteen. I also attended the Coventry City School of Excellence for a year.

What senior teams did you play for?

My first team was Racing Club Warwick at sixteen I played for them up to when I went to university aged nineteen. I played for Leamington after university whilst in a gap year. Then when I was teaching in Milton Keynes I played for Wootton Blue Cross (one season in the Spartan South Midlands Premier League), Biggleswade Town (two years) (Southern Football League, Division One Central then Leighton Town (three years) Southern Football League (Evo-Stik League Southern) Division One Central.

Did you enjoy your time with Leamington; it must have been a great time to be there?

I loved playing at Leamington! We had an awesome team which was just a team full of friends basically. Cadzy was manager and he just made everything fun, plus we won almost all the games which always helps. It was just an exciting time to be at the club with everything starting back up gain. It was really nice to play our home games at the Windmill too.

When did you join Westlea and how long were you at the club?

I joined the club when I was sixteen and played for them basically till I went off to university at nineteen. Then I lived in Milton Keynes and then

Singapore, if I was back home in Kenilworth I would always call Ash and Bagar up to get involved.

Tell me a bit about your time with Westlea, do you have any favourite matches, which players stood out for you?

I was sixteen and playing for Racing Club Warwick in the Southern League with Dave Draper as manager (1996-1998). Drapes wanted me to get used to adult football a bit more so he invited me to come along and play for them on Sundays. We had a great team and lots of the players also played for Racing Club Warwick. Being part of Westlea is like being part of an extended football family. Even though haven't lived in England since 2011, I know I can always call them up and get involved in whatever way.

My favourite match would be against a Balsall Common team. It was just a league game but I played centre mid and just really enjoyed it. Plus we won about 8-0.

Players that stood out were Brian Agar - such an intelligent player, the Walker brothers - always as solid as a rock and more recently I've always been really impressed with Josh Cole and Luke Cole.

Thanks for your time Nick.

Curly O'Callaghan

I have become friends with Curly on Facebook but I have known about him for a number of years through his work in local football.

Curly is a Leamington kid and big fan of the Brakes since he was six years old. Curly has fond memories of when he was a mascot for one of the FA Cup matches against Southend in the 1970s. When Curly was a kid he lived in Windmill Road next to the old ground and on Tuesday and Thursday evenings when AP were training he would ask Knoxy for a game. This brought back memories of my uncle Alan who grew up on Windmill Road telling me when they used to sneak into the old ground. Curly knows Barry Reeve (Leamington FC kit man) Barry is my Uncle Fred's brother in law it is a small world!

As a player Curly played for Westlea Wanderers but excelled as a manager of Stockton, Southam, Racing Club Warwick, Woodford, Redditch and Leamington Youth Team

Curly is a big fan of the AP Leamington sides of the 1970s and 1980s, I asked him to name his favourite squad

Goalkeepers - Vince O'Keefe, Jason Pearcey

Defenders - Dennis Taylor, Len Derby, Alan Jones, Roger Brown, Ian Britton

Midfield - Ivor Talbot, Micky Boot, Tommy Gorman

Forwards - Mick Keeley, Errington Kelly, Kim Casey, Duncan Gardner, Adrian Stewart

Jimmy Knox The Gaffer!

There are certainly some talented players and goals in that squad.

In May 2011 A Coventry City 1987 FA Cup winning XI played against a Curly select XI in a charity match at Leamington FC. A day which Curly remembers well as a lot of money was raised for charity.

Curly is a true fighter he has battled chronic lymphocytic leukaemia, this year he has had a transplant and chemotherapy. Everybody is rooting for you Curly you are a battler stay strong. Thank you for sharing your football memories with me.

Current team

At the time of writing Westlea Wanderers are running away with Division One of the Tracey Thomas Leamington and District Sunday League. Westlea opened the season with a 4.0 win over Khalsa on 8th September 2019 then followed up by a 5.0 win away at Leamington Hibernians. Westlea beat Heathcote 5.0 at the end of September; October saw wins over Napton, Leamington Old Boys and The Engine in league and cup competitions.

The result of the season so far is an impressive 10.1 win over Kineton on 3rd November 2019, a hat rick from Brady Floyd, two from Martin Hutchcox. Powell, Wright, Jervis and O'Loughlin also scored.

Westlea have strength in depth this season, striker Adam Knight recruited from Bishop's Tachbrook. They also have - Craig Watkin, Ciaran Houston, Luke Cole, Scott Hammond, Neil Stacey, Henry Leaver, Jake Montgomery, George Ayley Josh Cole and Jamie Coleman and Sean Castleton. I follow Westlea's results on the Facebook group, thank you to Michael Ellis and whoever admins this group. Chris Walker is usually one of the first to say well done lads! After fifty five years the team is still going strong, credit to the management team and players for this. Hopefully see them a win few more trophies at the end of the season. It is fantastic that this great club is still going strong, may it continue for years to come.

Chapter Two – Leamington Saturday and Sunday League teams

We are now going to have a look at some of the great Leamington teams over the years.

Khalsa

Leamington Khalsa was formed in 1965 and is one of the longest running teams in the area. Founder member Biker Singh is still very much involved to this day.

Gurpreet Dosanjh

I spoke to Gurpreet on the phone; Gurpreet is Biker Singh's son. Biker came to Leamington from India aged thirteen in the 1960s along with a few mates they formed a team and called themselves 'Indian Boys' and they contacted the league secretary to enter the league. With the support of the local temple they became Leamington Khalsa and have gone on to become an established team in Leamington football.

Biker in his playing days was a winger; Gurpreet described him as an 'Indian Maradona'. Biker has dedicated most of his life to Khalsa who have gone from strength to strength establishing teams in different age groups and other sporting teams. Gurpreet told me that they played in tournaments across the country; football brought different communities together and built positive relationships.

Gurpreet himself played for twenty years for Leamington Hibs and Khalsa, a midfield ball winner he had trials for Racing Club Warwick. Now living in London he used to work for an MP and now teaches Yoga. Gurpreet spoke with pride of what his dad has achieved with Khalsa.

Khalsa basically means community, in other parts of the midlands other teams were set up GNG FC in Leicester and Sporting Khalsa (West Midlands). GNG FC is a similar story to Leamington Khalsa.

Leamington Khalsa Juniors Football Club was founded in 1992 and now has teams in every age group from five to seventeen. The club is now one of the largest multi-cultural football clubs in the midlands with many players from non-Asian background. Volunteer coaches have included ex professionals Mark Walters and David Phillips.

In 2016 Leamington Khalsa's adult team won the Boyd Carpenter Charity Cup and the Andy Campbell Cup. Khalsa for some years have been one of the strongest teams in the Tracey Thomas Leamington and District Sunday League Division One. 2020 will mark fifty five years of Leamington Khalsa something that should be celebrated. The town of Leamington should be very proud of what Biker Singh has achieved, may the success continue for years to come.

Jet Kang

I contacted Jet via Facebook and email, Jet and his brother Shandy were both good players in local football.

Could you tell me what Junior and senior teams that you played for and some of your memories of your playing days?

I began playing for Central Ajax from Under 10's in 1978 under the late Don Hemingway, becoming the captain for the under 11's to under 14's, playing for Brian Docker.

I then signed for Racing Club Juniors from under 15's through to men's level for three years. I played under manager Brian Knibb; we had changed names from Racing to Newbold Common Arms in the men's league for the last season I was there. I left to go to play for Khalsa in the 1986/87 season in the Sunday Premier League at the age of seventeen. I continued to play for Khalsa on Sundays until I hung up my boots around 2005.

I also Captained the Mid Warwickshire College team to the National Semi Finals losing to St Austell college having beaten several Midlands college teams to represent The Midlands, this was in the 1988/89 season.

I also played for Stoneleigh Arms on a Saturday around 1990/91 I then signed for Pottertons for two seasons after which I went to play for Cubbington Albion. The highlight of my time with Cubbington was beating Leamington Hibs in the Coventry League Saturday Charity Cup.

In that team I played alongside the likes of my brother Shandy Kang, Frank Cronin, "Diddy" Dave Guest, the three Coleman brothers, Rich Kinsey to name a few.

Could you tell me a little bit about Shandy's career? I believe that he played with Billy Jawandha at Cubbington Albion in the late 1970s.

Yes Shandy was in that same team with Billy and also played for Racing Club on Saturdays in the mid to late 80's/ early 90's. He was signed by Wolves as an apprentice at sixteen and Captained Birmingham County, playing with the likes of Gary Shaw of Villa!!

He also played for the County and Region and different age levels and also played for Coventry Sporting!!

Obviously he played at Khalsa before and with me and also Cubbington as you say before and with me too.

Thanks for sharing those memories Jet.

Tony' Banger' Walsh

One of Khalsa's most famous players was Tony 'Banger' Walsh who was a goalkeeper. Tony is well known as a wrestler but back in the 1960s and 1970s he played in goal for Khalsa and Bishop's Tachbrook. In them days he was known as John Sheehan. Tony ran the Jack and Jill / Half Nelson in Lillington he also played in goal for their Sunday league team. A Former

Coventry City vice-president, Tony has been a keen Sky Blues fan over the years.

Tony often played in showbiz teams, he met close friend Eddie Kidd in a showbiz match. In 1985 Tony blew the whistle on wrestling giving away some of the secrets, in the 1970s and 1980s wrestling was very popular. I remember as kid watching Tony on World of Sport, often in a tag team against Big Daddy. Since retiring from wrestling, Tony has run his own security firms and has been an after dinner speaker.

Kebby Dhesi

Kebby was one of Khalsa's best players from the 1970s, below is a selection of his goal scoring through the decade.

23rd October 1971

Khalsa got top of Division Five

Kebby Dhesi scored a hat rick as Khalsa beat Thornbank Students 4.1, Kebby has now scored ten goals this season.

15th January 1972

Khalsa score sixteen goals

Khalsa scored an incredible sixteen goals in a Division Five 16.1 win over Lilywhites reserves. Surbjit Singh scored four goals, three each for Nirmal Singh, Armajit Avjule and Kebby Dhesi.

6th November 1976

Impressive from Khalsa

Khalsa beat Long Itchington 5.4 away in the Leamington Sunday League Premier Division. Kebby Dhesi with three goals, one each for Gurnam Aujla and Ranbir Singh. Long Itchington's goals were scored by Roger Constable, Mick Palis and John Woodhouse.

4th November 1978

Khalsa win battle of top two

Khalsa beat Kineton 2.1 to go top of Division One thanks to two goals from Kebby Dhesi

Leamington Southend

Leamington Southend had very good Saturday and Sunday teams in the 1960s and 1970s. Notable players include Mick Collins, Johnny Bull, Ivor Talbot, Billy Shanahan, Keith Jones, Roger Talbot, Pepe Gill, Derek Haggitt, Dennis Haggitt, Ian Claridge and Eric Canning

Malcolm Jukes

Malcolm was a goalkeeper for Leamington Southend; I contacted him on Facebook and asked him a few questions.

How long did you play for Leamington Southend for and what other teams did you play for?

I was sixteen when I started playing for Southend on a Sunday and AP Works on a Saturday. Prior to that I played for Lillington Dynamos and Warwick West End. I was with Southend for three seasons then I played Rugby, great times and great characters.

There were some great players in Sunday league, which players stood out in particular?

That is a difficult question because they all had their individual talents and there wasn't a bad player amongst them. However Billy Shanahan a centre half always looked after me because I was the youngest and he wasn't particularly quick, but not much got past him, if you know what I mean he was like a Tommy Smith of Liverpool. Up front we had two exceptional players in Johnny Bull (Bully) and Alan Bryant (Lollipop) I admired Alan because he was an old fashioned centre forward big strong route one type of guy who took no notice of reputations. Finally our little midfield dynamo Keith Jones, he was quick and skilful and could read the game. I would liken him to Alan Ball.

Thank you very much Malcolm.

Alan Bryan

I contacted Alan via Facebook; he was a good centre forward in local football.

Alan went to Campion School in Leicester Street he played junior football for Whitnash Warriors alongside Dave Garratt. Alan was a big centre forward who played Sunday League football for Avon Star, Leamington Southend and Long Itchington (for about eight seasons in the 1970s). Alan told me "Westlea were our bogie team I think I've got about five or six runner up medals to them but we had quite a good record in cup finals against them". "Nat Whitlock was my favourite centre forward". Alan played for AP Leamington briefly under Jimmy Knox but it was a step up to high! He also played for Stratford Town and Racing Club Warwick.

I asked Alan what he thinks the best side he played in, Alan told me he had two years with Radford United in the Coventry and North Warwickshire League. "We had a good team under manager John Butler we were runners up then champions and won the Coventry City Cup both seasons".

The nickname Lollipop came from John Bull's dad at PM Hopkins, he caught him leaning on his shovel while mixing. Shouting across the room Alan stop lolloping about! The nickname then stuck, it's varied over the years.

Whittle Wanderers

Formed in 1968 by a group of mates at the Jet and Whittle pub in Brunswick Street. Whittle Wanderers were to become a force in Sunday football in a few years. One of the mates was Tom Lewin who got interested in football going to Tech with Bob Phillips and Chris Elliott who both became very good players. Tom also helped out at Warwick Juniors; together with Dar Singh and Malc Coop (no relation to Mick) they came up with the idea to form a football team.

Whittle Wanderers were beaten 12.0 by Southam United in their first match in 1968 which was a friendly; this is how they lined up.

Pete Harris, Dar Gill, Tom Lewin, Roger Constable, Tim O'Connor, Ogger Meades, Malc Coop, Danny Harris, John Bolitho, Ernie Constable, Colin Richardson

In 1976/77 Whittle Wanderers had a very strong squad of players many would play at a good standard of football.

Whittle Wanderers - Roper, Talbot, Coles. Glenn, Draper, Stacey, Tomkins, Morby, Coleman, Middleton, McKinley, Garner, Hill, Phillips, Dyer, Clarke, Hardy, Carden, Guinane

Kelvin Evans

I contacted former Whittle Wanderers left back Kelvin on Facebook and asked him a few questions about his career. Kelvin is a former pupil of Campion School a couple of years below Eddie Hemmings and David Woodfield.

Could you tell me about how you got into football and what teams you played for?

I didn't play competitive football until my last year at school in 1966, before that every night behind the Jack and Jill pub in Lillington. I was football mad, I signed for Leamington St Marys at sixteen with Trevor Prestige, Alan Bryan and Dave Cramp R.I.P. There were some right characters there 'Smudger' Smith, Dave Wickes, Dabber Broughton R.I.P. I then played for Leamington Celtic Sunday youth team run by Jim Barry. Leamington Celtic had the pick of the area, a great team.

I played for men's football for Leamington Celtic, Whittle Wanderers, Bishop's Itchington, Bishop's Tachbrook, Radford Semele, FC Royals. I flirted with higher stuff with Racing Club Warwick, Southam and Coventry Amateurs but I liked a laugh and a pint rather than the serious stuff. Hence playing for where I worked Thwaites, B&B trailers.

I played with various very talented locals like Dennis Farr, Alan Bryan, Roger Constable, to name a few I could go on forever but the one that always stands out for me is Ian walker what a player he was!

I played for the Hope Tavern and The Queens Head in my forties. It kept me involved and relatively fit.

Thank you for sharing these memories Kelvin.

Pete Roper

I contacted Pete via Facebook and email, he told me a bit about his Sunday League career. Pete was one of the best goalkeepers in local football in the late 1970s.

Could you tell me about your career Pete and some of your favourite memories?

I started at aged sixteen at Leamington Postal in the Premier Division (First Division as it was then known) for two seasons - 1972 to 1974. I then moved to Midland Sports when Leamington Postal folded - 1974 –1976. I joined Whittle Wanderers after turning down Westlea Wanderers and Leamington Southend - Ollie Guinane persuaded me to choose Whittle

Wanderers. I can't remember when Tachbrook Whittle folded (there is a thread here) possibly 1982 and I moved to Radford United then onto Westlea Wanderers Reserves in 1985.

I played mainly in the reserves in the beginning at Westlea but then established myself in the first team. I stopped playing in 1996 at the age of forty one, the season after Westlea won the Premier Division.

Pete also played Saturday football for Warwickshire County Council, Stratford Town and Southam United.

Pete told me regarding Stratford Town, that there were a few Leamington based players in Billy Shanahan, Keith Jones, Alan Bryan and Ivor Talbot. A couple of Stratford based players I recall in Mick Collett and Stuart Dixon. It was really a poor squad for that standard though and we were regularly well beaten that season.

I had a couple of stints at Southam United, the first time when they were in the Coventry and North Warwickshire league and later in the veteran stage of my career. They were in the Midland Combination League. I really enjoyed playing in both teams as they were basically the Long Itchington Sunday league team.

Players that stood out there were loads of them! Roger Constable, Mick Palis, Merv Hammond and Roy Brabrook were one of the best defensive lines I've played behind. John Woodhouse was such a frustrating player to play against, but what a talent. The two Simpsons - Ian, Keith and Kevin Lloyd

I have to admit I enjoyed both my stints at Southam United, talented players and great camaraderie. After my first stint at Southam, I turned out for a few clubs as you could sign on for multiple clubs so long as they played in different leagues - Radford United, Bishop's Tachbrook, WCC Staff, and Pottertons

I can't remember being on the winning side of the Cancer cup in the 1970's.I played for WCC Staff against Westlea in 1975, and for Whittle against Long Itchington and Westlea.

The Whittle side was certainly talented, but in the 70s the most talented side I played for was my Saturday team Warwick's County Council Staff. We surprised a lot of people in 1975 when we got through to the Cancer Cup final.

Before joining WCC Staff, I played for Jim Barry's sides - Avon Rovers, St Peters Celtic and Leamington Hibs (I was a member of the original team when Hibs was first formed after St Peters chucked us out to concentrate on youth football)

Thanks for your time Pete.

Chapter Three – The legends

Warwick Town legend

Ray Bethell

I had the pleasure of speaking to Ray on the phone. A centre half or full back, Ray was part of a good Warwick Town team of the 1950s that won the Warwickshire Combination League. Ray played school football for Shrubland Street and recalls playing with a Blackaby who may have been my uncle. As a young man Ray was in the Navy based at Bramcote near Nuneaton. Ray played in a good Lockheed Leamington junior team with Bill Draper, one match they played against a Birmingham Youth side and were 3 nil down at half time. A stirring comeback in the second half and they triumphed 4.3 the "Leamington Shakers" was the headline. Ray recalls Les Latham, Frank Gardner, Joey Watson and Bill Branston at Lockheed. In the 1950s Warwick Town enjoyed a town rivalry with Saltisford Rovers in which Ray recalls Warwick Town often won these matches. A particular memorable game for Warwick Town was beating Kenilworth Rangers 2.1 to stop them winning the league. Ray scored the winner and also scored Kenilworth's goal (own goal). Warwick Town reached the Camkin Cup final but lost to West Bromwich Albion B team, The Baggies included David Burnside who is famous for his ball-juggling abilities. David once entertained the crown at half time in a friendly against Russian team CDSA Moscow. Ray remembers Frank White who was a trainer with Warwick Town, Frank starred for Coventry City in the 1930s. Another great Warwick born player was Ernie Ward who Ray remembers going to Coventry City, Ernie would become a Lockheed Leamington legend. Ray also played for Stratford Town and Flavels before finishing at thirty two; he played rugby for Lockheed until he was forty five. Ray spoke highly of players Dave Montgomery, Hugh Morrow, Ivor Powell, Micky Stowe and Frank Gummery. At the age of eighty nine Ray lives in Whitnash and plays bowls with Les Woodfield brother of Wolves player David. A couple of years ago on holiday in Greece a chap came up to him and said are you Ray Bethell? I remember watching you as a kid! He also lived in Whitnash.

It was great to speak to you Ray, please keep in touch.

Sunday League legends

The 1960s and 1970s was a golden era for local football; we are now going to have a look at some of the legends of this era.

Dave Garratt

Dave was one of AP Leamington's best goalkeepers in the 1970s, along with winger Ivor Talbot at one point they were the only local lads in the side. Dave was always a goalkeeper he played for his school teams Oken and Myton from 1964 to 1969 then various junior teams Binswood Athletic, Whitnash Warriors and Leamington St Johns. In 1969 he played for senior team South Leamington then he played Sunday League football for Westlea Wanderers. In 1973 Dave signed for AP Leamington and played for The Brakes for four years, during this time they played in the Southern League Premier Division. AP Leamington had some fine players in the mid-1970s; Dave told me that Roger Brown and Alan Jones were probably the best pair of central defenders in the league. In 1976 AP Leamington signed a certain Harry Redknapp however he didn't play that many games for The Brakes. Dave played against some famous players back then including Jimmy Greaves, Nigel Spink, Geoff Hurst, Derek Dougan, Jeff Astle and Ian Storey-Moore. Dave later played for Solihull Borough and Racing Club Warwick he also played cricket at a very good standard.

Dave told me when he joined Westlea in 1969 and played in the second team for a few years then made it to the first team in the 1971/72. He played for three full seasons until AP Leamington stopped him playing on Sundays due to contract. Dave did play a few games in 1974/5 and 1975/6 seasons, when allowed for match practice or following an injury. Dave is still really into his cricket and attended the Ashes at Edgbaston this summer, thank you for all your help Dave.

Dave is a really nice man I have met him for Coffee with Syd Hall and Ken Brown. It is a pleasure to include you this book.

Dennis Woodhead

I had the pleasure of speaking to Dennis on the phone, One of Westlea Wanderers greatest centre forwards. Dennis attended Oken High School and was in the same age group as Mick Coop, Ian Walker, Dennis Farr, and Barry Whitlock. Eddie Hemmings (England cricketer) went to Campion School he was the same year as Dennis and they often played against each other. In the late 1960s Dennis and Eddie were teammates at Pottertons FC. Dennis also played for Leamington Boys Club and he was one of the founder players of Westlea Wanderers.

Pottertons FC played in the Coventry Works League in the 1969/70 season they had some good players. Former Lockheed Leamington left winger of the 1950s George Burrows played for them. Dennis talked about Geoff Meakin and Bobby Phillips. Teammate Chris Woodhead was no relation to Dennis.

Dennis also played for Winsams, Warwickshire County Council and Stratford Town but is more famous for his twenty years playing for Westlea Wanderers. A famous match was in March 1972 when Westlea Wanderers hammered Bearley United 15.2 with Dennis scoring ten goals. Dennis recalls" it was one of those games where everything went right, as a centre forward at times you have to be a little greedy. I could have scored even more that day possibly twelve" Dennis told me it was a team effort and wouldn't have scored so many without great players around him. When Winsams folded Westlea became the dominant side in Leamington Sunday football. Keith Orme and Barry Whitlock joined Westlea from Winsams; Dennis often played at centre half when Barry signed.

Dennis goes for trial at Nuneaton Borough

Dennis impressed Nuneaton Borough manager David Pleat and went on trial at Manor Park and played in a couple of Midland Floodlit Cup matches. Dennis scored two goals against Bedford Town, in his first game against Telford he assisted Trevor Shepherd for his goal but Borough lost 3.1. Brakes fans will recognise Ernie Wilkinson, Alan Jones and Jimmy Goodfellow who all played for AP Leamington. Nuneaton Borough was then playing in the Southern League Premier Division and also had a young Kirk Stephens on their books. Trevor Shepherd previously played for Coventry City as did Gerry Baker who was also at Nuneaton Borough then. Scottish born Gerry played international football for USA, his older brother Joe played for England. David Pleat wanted Dennis to play more for Nuneaton but due to work and family it wasn't viable for Dennis.

Nuneaton Borough v Telford United 16-03-1972

Nuneaton Borough: Edwards, Tedds, Jones, Newbury, Gill, Wilkinson, Shaw, Goodfellow, Woodhead, Shepherd, Harris.

Telford beat Nuneaton 3.1 in this Midland Floodlit Cup match; however Dennis assisted Trevor Shepherd for the equalising goal.

Dennis talked about some of the great players of that era, he rated Syd Bench very highly he was a fine full back. Ian Walker was a leader a class player who was a certainly good enough to play for Coventry City. John Rose, Keith Gould, Chris Elliott, Dave Garratt and Malc Hyland were all good players. Roger Constable, Ian Claridge, Billy and Dony Shanahan were good opponents. When Dennis finished playing with Westlea he played for Whitnash "The first time I got booked was against Westlea playing for Whitnash"

Dennis and his brothers were a sporting family; Dennis also played Tennis, Table Tennis, Rugby, Cricket and athletics. Now retired he lives in Whitnash and often goes to Brakes matches.

Two Dennis Woodhead's

Fans who remember football in the 1950s would have heard of Dennis Woodhead of Sheffield Wednesday. Dennis is Dennis's uncle (Dennis's dad's brother) the family originated from Sheffield.

Dennis the elder was born in Hillsborough, Sheffield on 12th June 1925. Dennis's grandfather was Billy Betts a left half who played for Wednesday FC and once for England in 1889.

Dennis played football and cricket for Sheffield Boys, after leaving school he played for works team Edgar Allen Tools. In April 1945 he signed professional forms for Sheffield Wednesday, during the war years he served in the RAF. Dennis played mainly as a left winger sometimes centre forward, his Owls career began in 1947 after leaving the RAF. The early 1950s was a successful time for Sheffield Wednesday, two promotions to the First Division. The Owls had a few talented players in that era - Derek Dooley and England internationals Jackie Sewell, Albert Quixall Redfern Froggatt. Dennis played 213 times scoring 73 goals before joining Chesterfield in 1955 then had spells with Derby County and Southport. In May 1959 Dennis retired from full-time League football. Dennis played a bit of non-league football as a player-manager for Frickley Colliery and Retford Town. From 1971 to 1987 he was Commercial Development Officer at Sheffield Wednesday, he sadly passed away on 26 July 1995 aged seventy.

It was a pleasure speaking to Dennis who speaks fondly of the golden era of Sunday football; there were so many great players back then when football was really enjoyable. Thank you for your time Dennis and hopefully see you at a Leamington match.

Barry 'Nat' Whitlock

Born in Althorpe Street in Royal Leamington Spa on 9th September 1945, Barry went to Campion School for Boys in Leicester Street. Barry played Saturday football for South Leamington, Lockheed Works, and Saltisford Rovers who became Racing Club Warwick then joined Lockheed Leamington in the summer of 1971. A Sunday league legend with Winsams and Westlea Wanderers Barry was a prolific striker. In the 1970/71 season Barry scored twenty nine goals for Racing Club Warwick the next season for Lockheed he scored twenty two goals. Barry re-joined Racing Club after Lockheed appointed Jimmy Knox as manager; his appearances were limited under Knox.

Leamington Sunday League 1968/69 season Barry scored 43 goals for Winsams which they won the league by two points. 1969/70 season Barry scored 34 goals Winsams won the league again.

After Winsams folded Barry joined Westlea Wanderers he once scored four goals in a Midland Sunday League Cup match against Nuneaton league champions Church Road WMC. Barry also played for Leamington Celtic and Whittle Wanderers.

Dennis Farr

Dennis was one of the most prolific strikers in local football in the late 1960s and early 1970s.

In the 1969/70 Leamington Sunday League season he helped Winsams to the title; Dennis scored twenty six goals and formed a potent partnership with Barry Whitlock.

Dennis was at trial at Coventry City and Wolverhampton Wanderers also showed an interest in him. In 1967 he played a couple of games for Lockheed Leamington in the Midland Floodlit Cup. Dennis was a great goal scorer for North Leamington and Saltisford Rovers/Racing Club Warwick he also played for Worcester City Reserves and Claverdon Old Boys. Like Ian Walker injury prevented him from playing at a higher level, Dennis was a natural finisher him and Barry together must have frightened the hell out of opposing defenders.

Dennis in the news

21st January 1967

Farr on target again

Free scoring North Leamington striker Dennis Farr scored three goals as they beat AP Works 4.1. Dennis has scored an incredible forty five goals in fifteen games.

23rd August 1969

Farr gets hat trick

Dennis scored three goals as Saltisford Rovers hammered Tipton 5.2

22nd February 1971

Late brace for Farr

Dennis scored two late goals as Racing Club Warwick beat Bilston Reserves 4.1. Whitlock and Denholm also scored.

<u>Duncan Gardner</u>

Duncan was a quality striker in the mid to late 1970s; he famously scored ten goals for Westlea Wanderers in 1977 against Albion Athletic. Duncan told me " I remember going up to Coventry City's training ground to have a photo taken with Ian Wallace and Mick Ferguson (Coventry City strike partners) trying to hold ten footballs!! This was arranged by my old friend Roger Draper" Roger was Sports Editor at the Courier at that time. Duncan's father Eric played for Lockheed Leamington in the 1940s he used to come and watch Duncan at the Old Windmill. Duncan's form in particular in the FA Cup for AP Leamington attracted interest from league clubs and he nearly signed for FA Cup first round opponents Torquay United. Duncan also played for Racing Club Warwick, Telford United, Nuneaton Borough, Worcester City and VS Rugby he had a second spell at Leamington in 1988 and scored in the clubs last ever league game on 16th April 1988 in a 2.2 draw v Walsall Wood.

Hi Duncan could you tell me about your memories of playing for Westlea Wanderers and your time in football?

I have fond memories of my time at Westlea indeed as it due to them that I went on to have a long semi pro career. I went to Westlea having played for Ford Sports and St Dominic's in the Leamington Sunday League and joined with a few 'mates' that I had played with at the other clubs mentioned as well as Pottertons. People like Tony Sollis (a lifelong friend from an early age), Cliff Morby, Mick Clarke, Terry Dyer, Paul Garner and

I'm sure there were others that I haven't mentioned.

There were several 'legends' already at Westlea at that time such as Ian Walker, Chris Elliot, Dennis Windsor, Ken Lambert, Ian Montgomery and it was a pleasure to play alongside them. Initial rivalry was against teams like Whittle Wanderers and Long Itchington and they were always great games played with passion and skill on both sides.

A couple of games still stand out such as the one where I scored the ten goals and also when we reached the final of the Birmingham Junior Cup where we lost 2-1 to Birmingham Rail at the old Coventry Sporting Club ground at Kirby Corner in Coventry. I also remember the many happy hours spent after the games at the Leopard Pub where the game was dissected over a few pints!

My non-league career got under way after 'Monty' recommended me to the then Racing Club Warwick manager (George Anderson) as they had a busy end of season schedule and needed a few players to help out. I played in an away match in Birmingham (I can't remember where) and we won 3-0 and I had quite a good game. George invited me to pre-season training and after playing in the first five or six league games for Racing and scoring quite a few goals, Jimmy Knox came along from AP and that was that.

I still maintain that the side I played in at Westlea would more than have held their own in a higher standard league on a Saturday at that time such as the Midland Combination. Great memories and thanks for reminding me of them.

I keep in touch with Duncan via email, at the time of writing Duncan is currently in Australia with England's over 60 Cricket team. Duncan helped England beat New Zealand and has played in four of the seven matches so far.

Ian Walker

Ian is one of Leamington Spa's greatest ever players, a legend of Westlea Wanderers and Racing Club Warwick. A class player, Ian could play in defence or midfield he played junior football for Milverton Villa and Oken High School. When Ian left school he was on the books of Coventry City along with friends Mick Coop and Dennis Farr. Ian suffered a serious injury which ended his chances of becoming a professional footballer, Mick went onto to become a legend at Coventry City I know that Ian would have too. At the age of sixteen in 1965 Ian along with friends Keith Gould, Bobby Timms, Keith Chamley, Gerald Pratt, Andy Curtlin, Dave Miles and Alan Jones formed Westlea Wanderers.

I spoke to Ian's wife Chris, she is very proud that Westlea Wanderers are still going after fifty five years and still a strong team in Leamington Sunday league football. Ian formed Leamington's greatest ever Sunday League team and was one of the best players in the golden era of Sunday League football in the 1960s and 1970s.

The Walker family legacy is continuing to this day, Chris's grandsons are on the books of Birmingham City their dad and Chris's son in law is Simon Rea who is a Kenilworth lad played as a central defender for Birmingham City and Peterborough United. Chris's sons Ashley and Simon were both good players who both played for Westlea. Simon (Walker) made 87 appearances for Leamington at left back or in central defence between 2001 and 2005. Chris's brother Ken was a good goalkeeper so the family certainly has football in its blood.

Ian also played for AP Works FC; in the late 1970s they had a good Saturday team. Ian played with Westlea teammates Don Grantham and Keith Orme for AP Works they also had Roger Talbot, Paddy Hardy and Keith Billington in the team.

Ian was also manager of Bishop's Tachbrook; during his time with the club he suffered his first brain tumour. Ian sadly passed away in 1995 he was forty six; Chris told me that the parish church was packed out for his funeral over 1500 people. Everyone that I spoke to who knew Ian spoke so highly of him as a player and as a person.

Ian in the news

12th October 1967

Westlea Wanderers beat Tesco

Ian Walker playing at inside left scored two goals as Wanderers beat Tesco 2.0 in a Leamington Sunday League Division One match.

15th May 1969

Walker and Rose represent Westlea in League XI

Ian Walker and John Rose have been selected to play for a Leamington Sunday League XI to play a match against Cardiff Combination at the Windmill ground.

Hyland (Lockheed Apprentices) Connor (Winsams) Keen (Winsams) Orme (Winsams) Walker (Westlea Wanderers) Cramp (St Dominic's) Rose (Westlea Wanderers) Whitlock (Winsams) Montgomery (St Dominic's) Talbot (Leamington Southend) Phillips (Leamington Southend)

Ian played briefly for Lockheed Leamington in 1967 when a number of local players played in the Floodlit Cup.

12th September 1970

Captain fantastic

Racing Club Warwick has enjoyed an unbeaten start to the West Midland First Division. One of the biggest factors in the clubs great start to the season is the form of skipper Ian Walker. Ian was captain of South Leamington in the Coventry and North Warwickshire League last season. Roy Bradley the brother of Racing Club Warwick manager Brian Bradley has been impressed by Walker. Roy who played for Lockheed said Ian has brilliant ball control and can hit an accurate pass from either foot; he has made a tremendous difference to the defence.

18th September 1971

Eight second half goals for Westlea

Westlea Wanderers hammered Leamington St Mary's thanks to three goals from Dennis Woodhead and two each for Ian Walker and Mick Chimes.

25th October 1971

Racing Club shock leaders

Racing Club Warwick inflicted Warley Borough's first West Midland League defeat of the season. Steve Cooper scored the only goal of the game, but it was the Racers midfield which was a key factor in the win. Ian Walker, John Rose, Bob Phillips and Chris Elliott were dominant players, forwards Cooper and Dennis Farr had good games.

7th May 1977

AP Works edged in Semi Final

AP Works were narrowly beaten 1.0 in the Coventry Evening Telegraph Challenge Cup Semi Final by Morris. Ian Walker and Keith Orme had great games; Stewart Smith hit the woodwork for AP. Fred Robinson got the winning goal for Morris who will meet GEC in the final at Highfield Road.

A Tribute to Ian by Don Grantham

I was honoured to have Ian as one of my very closest friends during my formative years in local football; we met when I was fifteen years old. Westlea Wanderers under Ian's captaincy and leadership had just won the Birmingham Junior Cup, and were the top local side. I was thrilled to be asked to join the club, and benefitted hugely by playing with a group of immensely talented local footballers – arguably the most talented being Ian. His calm reading of the game, ability to see situations before others, and technical talent to receive and play the ball positioned him as one of the very top local players. In addition, his leadership and guidance, of both experienced and young inexperienced teammates enabled him to have significant influence in every game he played. At a personal level, Ian's guidance and coaching, before, during, and after games made me – and I am sure – many others, much better players. Ian was a hugely humble man, with a great sense of living for the day! His default was to strive to make others better, never focusing on himself. That said he was a vital part of every team he played in – always one of the first names on the team sheet.

His influence on Westlea Wanderers was immense. As founder, player, captain, manager he was a key part of the foundation Westlea was built upon; and as a man, someone who always put others before himself, always willing to help a friend. He was also a wonderful father to Simon, Ashley and Lisa, and one of the proudest, but most difficult speeches I ever made was to speak for him at Lisa's wedding. Public speaking was not being something Ian was fond of, making that speech may not have been a moment he would not have relished! But he would have been so proud of Lisa and his boys that day! So sad he wasn't there to see his daughter, so beautiful on her wedding day. I was proud to be his friend. He was taken far too young, and is sadly, sadly missed. Ian Walker was a special player, but an even more special man.

Cliff Morby

One of the best local players in the 1970s and 1980s Cliff could play full back or midfield. A quick attacking ball player and good passer he formed a great midfield partnership with friend Mick Clarke at Racing Club Warwick and VS Rugby.

A Leamington lad, Cliff lived in Denby Close Lillington and attended Dormer High School in Warwick. Cliff went to Mid Warwickshire College after leaving school to study his trade carpentry.

I spoke to Cliff's wife Wendy and asked her a few questions about Cliff.

Wendy met Cliff in the late 1980s through a friend in Rugby; Cliff had finished playing football and was playing for Old Laurentians Rugby team in the town. Cliff was a talented sportsman he represented Leamington and District Junior Table tennis team. As a young man he went to St George's Boys Club in Leamington with Mick Rainbow who was also a good player in local football. Cliff and Mick both played table tennis for St George's Boys Club, at a trial of Leamington and District Table Tennis Association a fifteen year old Cliff impressed everyone. Cliff played junior football for Ajax who had a number of talented youngsters in Paul Coleman, Mick Clarke and Pete Roper. At one time Fourth Division Northampton Town had four Ajax players on trial – Cliff Morby, Terry Hood, Paul Coleman and Clive Hopkins.

Wendy told me that Cliff spoke fondly of his time playing football, a talented young player who broke into Racing Club Warwick's team aged sixteen. Cliff also played for Stratford Town, VS Rugby, Midland Red, Whittle Wanderers, Ford Sports and Westlea Wanderers. Cliff and Wendy's sons now play football; the man of the match award is named after Cliff which is a lovely tribute. Cliff was an extremely talented carpenter he made Wendy's parents a log cabin for them to live in at the top of their garden. Wendy spoke fondly of the Westlea Wanderers 50th celebration in 2015; Cliff enjoyed meeting former teammates and sharing memories of their playing days. Cliff was taken from us suddenly at the age of sixty two in 2017 he is sadly missed by everyone who knew him but can be very proud of the person he was.

Cliff in the news

24th October 1970

Cliff wins set in juniors match

Cheltenham beat Leamington and District 9.1 in a junior Table tennis match, Cliff Morby won Leamington's only set

17th April 1972

A run out for sixteen year old Cliff Morby

Racing Club Warwick beat Tipton Town 2.0 thanks to goals from Ian Montgomery and Keith Orme. The match gave an opportunity for Cliff to play twenty minutes and the young player impressed with energetic running and nearly scoring with a header.

8th November 1975

Two penalties for Morby

Cliff Morby scored two penalties as Ford Sports drew 3.3 with Avon Borough in the Leamington League. Chris Lea also scored for Fords Sports, A goal from Graham Ulyatt and a brace from Dennis Durnian for Avon Borough.

24th January 1976

Near neighbours and Friends help Racing Club Warwick

Mick Clarke and Cliff Morby are playing prominent roles for the Racers, the youngsters live within yards of each other and their careers have taken the same path via Pottertons and Ford Sports. Racing Club Warwick manager Roy Bradley said Cliff is a terrific worker in midfield, he can play anywhere.

16th September 1978

Cliff helps Westlea earn a point

Westlea Wanderers drew 3.3 with FC Royal who lost their 100 % record in the Leamington League. Cliff Morby, John Rose and Chris Prophet scored for Westlea. Stewart Smith, Rich Turpin and Dave Cleaver with the goals for FC Royal.

VS Rugby

In the 1976/77 season at VS Rugby under Lockheed Leamington legend Syd Hall, they had a number of Leamington and Warwick connections. Defenders - Billy Shanahan and Ken Sanders, in midfield Cliff Morby, Mick Clarke and Brian Barraclough. Forwards included Mick Berry, Stewart Gallagher and Ivor Talbot.

A tribute to Cliff by Chris Prophet

Chris played with Cliff at three different clubs Racing Warwick VS Rugby and Westlea Wanderers. "Cliff was the best player I ever played with! He had the tenacity of a Jack Russell and the skill and football brain of any midfield general. He was leader by pure example and encouraged commitment on everyone on the park. A great character off the pitch too and someone you would want alongside you in the trenches"

A tribute to Cliff by Don Grantham

Cliff was a hugely talented full back. Deceptively quick, with fantastic technical skills. His ability to bring the ball under control with one touch, and see and pick out a pass to well-placed colleagues made him a talent in demand in local football. Cliff played at Whittle wanderers before moving to Westlea Wanderers, and becoming a cornerstone of both a successful team, picking up numerous local honours, and the backroom group the club could depend on year in year out.

At a personal level, Cliff had a huge sense of fun he was always quick with a comment to bring humour and good nature. Cliff was always a member of the team, and the club who could be relied upon, even in the most challenging of games and the most challenging of times. Cliff would to build morale both on and off the pitch. A wonderfully talented player and a good person.

Two legends

I never met Cliff or Ian or saw them play; I hope that I would have been friends with both of them. I hope that Cliff and Ian's family and friends have been able to draw some comfort on how much they were both so very much well thought of. Cliff and Ian are Leamington legends who were both fantastic players and men. It has been my genuine pleasure writing about both of them.

Ian Montgomery

Can I first ask how your career began, what junior sides did you play for?

My "career" started while at a rugby playing school when a group of us joined Cubbington Albion Juniors. They played in the Leamington Sunday youth league in the mid-60's up against the likes of Westlea Wanderers and

St Peter's Bosco who were the top sides. While playing for them I snuck into the "Albion's" Reserves on a Saturday and then the first team who were in the Warwickshire Combination, the forerunner of the Midland Combination I believe. When we became too old for that league some of us moved to St Dominic's in the Leamington Sunday league proper. On Saturday's I was invited to Lockheed Leamington who wanted to trial some local talent. On my first training day I met a young lad who had been released by Leicester City called Dennis Taylor who you may know! Man could he play, in midfield then, same as me so I soon realised how tough that was going to be. Still I managed to get a few games, mostly mid-week away in various far flung places of the Southern League! Keith Shrimpton was there too and was a great help to me another smashing bloke and good player. Most weeks though saw me playing for South Leamington in the Coventry and North Warwick's league, a good standard and very competitive. Around this time, Racing Warwick under Roy Bradley decided to tap into the pool of local talent, an inspired decision, and one which was going to reap rewards eventually.

Westlea Wanderers were a fantastic side, what do you put the success down to? The team was capable of competing at a higher level.

In 1970 I joined Westlea Wanderers and I am still there to this day and proud to be. I had played against this team for the last five years and knew all the players from previous encounters and played with some of them at Racing. Phil Hall was secretary and some canny old heads helping him, but the glue that held it all together was Ian Walker. We all knew Ian was the best player around but his demeanour and attitude to everyone was both friendly and inspirational. Add that to the fact that all the players were good, they played at a higher level on a Saturday than your average Sunday league player and therefore were training twice a week. This was a big advantage, we were fitter than most teams and our reactions were quicker on the pitch which gave us quite an edge. Don't get me wrong, it wasn't easy because we had many friends around that we played with on a

Saturday playing in rival sides who did the same. But not the whole team!! Another factor which helped at Westlea was we knew how to enjoy ourselves! It wasn't just a football team. The social side of Westlea Wanderers was well known and if you hadn't got tickets for our New Year's do by the end of October you were going to struggle to get in.

What other senior sides did you play for?

Saturday's saw me venture to Racing Warwick then off to VS Rugby when Syd Hall was in charge. I then went back to Racing with Dietmar Bruck, before heading off to Stratford Town where I joined Sid Keenan and his brother Liam. Now both these chaps had vast semi-pro experience with teams like Saltisford Rovers and Halesowen Town so they were no mugs, but they were so much fun to work with. I have to admit that many of my Saturdays wanderings were probably due to my not Seeing Eye to eye with coaches after a time and I wanted to play every week! I was thirty years old when I joined Stratford, still playing midfield, training twice a week and up for it .The following season, Sid and Liam asked me to play sweeper! Didn't fancy that much, but it seemed to work ok for the next seven years! This was my most enjoyable time in Saturday football I remember as we got back Stratford town's senior status and hopefully started them on the way to the success they achieved in later years. Last of all was a return to Racing, playing at first then becoming assistant manager to John Bettles and overseeing the rise of another team of local talent to win the Midland Combination and achieve promotion to the Southern League. That was something, local players playing attractive attacking football and winning. It certainly got the turnstiles ticking over.

Which players stand out when you were playing?

To pick out special players in this team would be an injustice. Everybody contributed and everyone joined in which made it all such a delight and a success. Over the years we have tried to keep the same formula as near as we can and continued the success. Of course we lost Phil Hall very early on and dear Ian in the mid-90's, such a tragedy, but people have stepped in , notably Neil Treadwell, Paul Garner, Keith Billington and for the last ten or so years Ian Billington and Ashley Walker to try and keep things going, hopefully this will continue

Here are a few names...…… Ian Walker, Chris Elliott, John Rose, Denis Woodhead, Denis Farr, Ajit Braich, Andy Townshend, Graham Ulyatt, Duncan Gardener, Keith Orme, Pepe Gill, Sid Bench, Don Grantham, Bill Shanahan, Alan Bryan. If this was a typewriter, I'd have to change the ribbon! Dave Garrett, Malc Hyland and Tony Partridge.

Monty the legend

I have contacted a number of former players from the 1960s and 1970s when I have asked which players stand out back in the day, Ian Montgomery is always mentioned. Ian was one of the most consistent players of that era; he is highly regarded in local football. Part of a great partnership with John Bettles at Racing Club Warwick, Ian's contribution as John's assistant was invaluable in the clubs success in the late 1980s. Thank you for sharing some of your memories with me Monty.

Tom Lewin

Tom is a local historian and author, I first heard of Tom when I bought a book which he co-wrote called Pubs of Royal Leamington Spa which is an excellent read. I further discovered that Tom wrote an article about Westlea Wanderers on the Leamington history group website in 2015 which was the 50th anniversary of the club forming. I have got to know Tom through Facebook and email he has been very helpful answering questions about local football.

Without Tom and his friends we wouldn't have had Whittle Wanderers, Tom has got another book out soon about Leamington shops which will definitely be worth a read. I hope Tom one day writes a book about local football he has so much knowledge to share.

Mike Berry

A local footballer who has become a successful sports writer, I contacted Mike via email.

Can I firstly ask you how you got into football, what junior teams did you play for?

I watched Lockheed Leamington from the mid-1960s on a regular basis ... my favourite player was the deadly Ray Holmes but I also had a soft spot for Syd Hall and Alan Vest. I actually saw Kevin Keegan score at the Windmill for Scunthorpe United Reserves in the late-1960s. I played at Lillington Junior School where I represented Mid-Warwickshire Schoolboys at eleven alongside Duncan Gardner, Paul Coleman and Mick Mackey (Ben's dad) but then I went to a rugby playing school Leamington College, so never played school football again. Instead I played Sunday junior football for Warwick West End between 1969 and 1972, scoring fifty two goals in 1971-72 as we won the league and cup double for the second successive season. Eric Overton, who later played for Brakes, was in goal and Roger Thomas, son of the legendary Tracey Thomas, also played. I was a big Leicester City fan and used to go to home and away Leicester games with the Thomas family.

What senior sides have you played for?

At sixteen I joined Thwaites (Leamington Sunday League Division Two) as my dad worked there for many years. My first game was on a wet Thursday night at Bury Road against B&B Trailers; we only had ten men and lost 12-1. By the end of the season we had won promotion and the League Cup (I scored 28 goals in 27 games including four second-half goals in the 5-1 win over Lilywhites in the League Cup final). I then joined Long Itchington, managed by my late Uncle Ollie - or Twisty as he was known. He was caretaker-manager of Brakes for one game in the 1980s. I had played for them in the Rugby Sunday League the previous season, playing for Thwaites on Sunday mornings, then Long Itchington on Sunday afternoons! We won promotion from Division One in the first season (I got 30 goals in 21 games including five in a 14-0 win over Thwaites!). The Long Itchington team of the day was dominated by the fantastic Constables. I played in games when six of the brothers played ... Roger, Ernie, Brian (aka Pancho), Colin, Paul and Dave. I also had a season with Banbury United in 1973-74, mainly for the reserves (scoring four hat-tricks in a six-game purple patch) but played the last few months in the first team, scoring with a diving header on my debut against Marlow and also playing in a 2-1 win over AP Leamington on Easter Monday (ironically one of my worst ever performances but it was my seventh game in thirteen days, a fixture pile-up caused by the power restrictions of the day). Brakes had won the Southern League Cup on the Saturday and we famously beat them with two Jim Hastie penalties in the last seven minutes. The next season I had injury problems (20 goals in 25 games for Long Itchington) and the following season I joined Westlea. I scored 20 in 21 games (also playing for AP youth team) before leaving in March 1976 when I joined VS Rugby (under Syd Hall, one of my early heroes and the man responsible for me joining Banbury) and signed a contract preventing me from playing on Sundays. Jimmy Knox tried to buy me off VS Rugby in November 1976 as a replacement for George Cleary (when Harry Redknapp was with the Brakes) but after having talks I stayed at Butlin Road. I probably should have signed ... though I really did enjoy playing for VS Rugby. Leicester City also showed an interest after I scored against them in a pre-season friendly (a 1-0 win) but nothing came of it. I also played for Cubbington Albion and Chrysler in the Coventry Alliance, Southam United in the Coventry and North Warwickshire League and Warwick West End briefly in the Stratford Alliance. I also spent the best part of a season with Shrewsbury Town as a sixteen year-old and proudly scored for Leicester City Youth in my one and only game for them.

What was your preferred playing position?

I played as both a centre-forward and out wide as a winger/striker. I preferred centre-forward as there was less tracking back!

Could you tell me a bit about your time with Westlea, memories, team-mates?

I had one season with them in 1975-76. Six of my goals came in the same game, an 11-1 Challenge Cup thrashing of Hampton Magna at St Nicholas Park in Warwick. I scored the winner against Whittle (1-0) on my debut and a hat-trick against Leamington Southend but the game I remember most vividly was a 3-3 draw with Whittle at Newbold Comyn. I scored what I consider my best goal for Westlea with a left-footed drive from way out on an angle and we were 3-1 up before Ollie Guinane levelled by completing a hat-trick and only a desperate foul prevented him from snatching a last-gasp winner. I had played with Ollie for Warwick West End senior side before joining Banbury; he was one of the great characters of Leamington football and a cracking bloke. It was a privilege playing with the likes of Ian Montgomery (in my opinion the best player to ever come out of Leamington), Chris Elliott (who I still see watching Stratford Town), Keith Orme, Syd Bench and the late Ian Walker at Westlea. Monty and Micky Rainbow also played for VS at the same time as me. As for opponents, Roger Constable was always a big challenge (thankfully I was on his side most of the time!) and a chap called Pete Deakin, who played for Ford Sports and Pottertons, also proved difficult, mainly because he used to wind me up.

Could you tell me about BACKPASS, how it all started and your writing career?

I first ran a small magazine called Sunday Soccer that featured Division Three of the Leamington Sunday League with some mates when I was thirteen ... my brother was playing for Burgis and Colbourne in the division at the time. Then when I gave up playing at twenty three to concentrate on journalism - I had a serious blood disease in 1978 that helped bring an end to my playing days - I ran another magazine featuring all of the Sunday League in 1980 called Sunday Football Focus. I then did the Sunday League Match of the Week in the Courier and have spent the last forty years covering football, cricket and speedway. I reported on the Brakes in the 1980s until they folded in 1988 - I was at the Poole game when they won the Southern League and the Gillingham FA Cup tie in 1983 (I stood behind the goal to watch the Southend FA Cup tie in 1974) and was on the committee that organised the final game at the old Windmill between Jimmy Knox's XI and Graham Allner's XI in 1988, also producing the programme. I then covered Northampton Town for 11 years (1987-1998) before working for the Daily Telegraph for eight years (doing Football League games, including the Premier League). I also covered Leamington's 9-1 defeat at Colchester in 2005 for the Coventry Evening Telegraph (I was the speedway correspondent of the CET from 1993 to 2006). I then started BACKPASS in 2007.

Don Grantham

I spoke to Don on the phone and asked him some questions about his football career. Don went to Cashmore School and was team captain when they won an under 11 trophy, after leaving Cashmore he went to Warwick Boys School. Between the ages of ten and sixteen he played for St Peters Celtic on Sundays, towards the end of his time there he got spotted by Ted Forde who was a friend of AP Leamington manager Jimmy Knox. Don played for AP Leamington's youth team which he enjoyed as he was a fan of the team. In the 1960s he used to watch Lockheed Leamington his favourite players were Ray Holmes, Syd Hall and Ernie Ward, Don lived near Tachbrook Road.

Ted (Forde) took Don to Coventry City and he played Sunday morning schoolboy football, Don was the year below Kenilworth lad Barry Powell. As a player Don had great control and stamina but didn't have much pace, in his early twenties he suffered a cartridge injury which prevented him becoming a professional player. At the age of fifteen he played for Westlea Wanderers, senior players Ian Walker and Malc Hyland were a good ten years older than Don. Westlea had some great players Don got to know Ian very well and became good friends, Pep Gill, Dennis Woodhead, Keith Gould, Chris Elliott all good players.

Don was in the same age group as Paul Coleman, Dave McMahon and Duncan Gardner, by the late 1970s they were all established players in local football.

Don in the news

6th December 1975

Westlea hammer Radford United

Don Grantham and Mick Rainbow both got two goals as Westlea Wanderers won 6.1. Dennis Woodhead and Mick Berry also scored, Brian Mathews with Radford's consolation goal.

23rd September 1977

New signing Don Grantham in squad of 13

Racing Club Warwick manager Gerry Baker names new signing from AP Works Don Grantham in a squad of 13 to face Raunds Town in the FA Vase.

Hyland, Newberry, Taylor, Evans, Cooper, Downing, Fisher, Randle, McGovern, Montgomery, Anderson, McGreener, Grantham

20th August 1979

New signings do well for Stratford

Don Grantham and Cliff Morby impressed for Stratford as they drew 2.2 with Mile Oak Reserves. Graham Uylatt and Steve Bradley scored for Stratford.

Chris Prophet

Chris got into football after he left school; he got taller when he left which helped him become a centre forward. I spoke to Chris on the phone and asked him about his football career. Chris is a Coventry kid from Walsgrave he went to Caludon Castle School with Kirk Stephens who went onto to become a professional footballer, a right back who played for Luton Town and Coventry City. As a youngster Chris was a ball boy for Coventry City during this time they were promoted to the First Division, he had a season ticket for many years.

Chris played junior football for GEC Coventry and Chrysler Staff then onto Westlea Wanderers on Sundays where he would play for fourteen years.

Chris was a centre forward who could hold the ball up, good in the air .Jimmy Knox the AP Leamington manager was looking at Chris and Duncan Gardner, Duncan was the best player he played up front with. In one match Duncan scored ten goals for Westlea, Chris made about nine of them. Chris and Duncan were the Toshack and Keegan of local football in the late 1970s. Duncan would sign for AP Leamington, Chris played at a good standard for Racing Club Warwick and VS Rugby he got a trial with Derby County under manager Tommy Docherty. Whilst at the Baseball Ground Chris played with Kevin Wilson who himself was from Banbury, he had a good career playing for Chelsea and Northern Ireland.

Chris talked about the many great players and managers around at the time in local football, Ian Montgomery, Cliff Morby, Ian Goodwin all stand out as great players he played with. Great managers included George Anderson (GEC and Racing Club Warwick), Syd Hall (VS Rugby) and Ian Walker (Bishop's Tachbrook). There were a lot of good characters in Leamington back then Billy Shanahan, Bobby Hancock's and Roger Constable.

Thank you for your time Chris and sharing your memories with me.

28th December 1977

Thriller as Prophet grabs three

Chris Prophet scored three goals as Racing Club Warwick beat Stratford Town 5.3. Stuart Fisher got a brace for the Racers. Alan Bryan, Keith Hancock and Ivor Talbot scored for Stratford.

There certainly have been some fantastic players in the 1960s and 1970s that were good enough to play professionally. I hope that you have enjoyed this chapter about the legends of local football.

Bob Phillips

One of the best midfielders in local football in the 1960s and 1970s, I spoke to Bob on the phone and asked him a few questions about his football career. Bob went to Oken High School and was part of their very good team of the early 1960s. Bob has great memories of this team, they were possibly the area's best ever school team. After Oken with some of the other lads, Bob played for Avon Rovers under 18s. On 3rd May 1966 Avon Rovers beat Coventry City Juniors 1.0 to win the Coventry Junior Cup. Bob scored the winning goal at the Butts Stadium in Coventry, he recalls playing against a young Jeff Blockley and one of the reserves was Willie Carr. Both Jeff and Willie went onto become full internationals so it certainly goes to show that Avon Rovers had a good side. Bob played a few games for Lockheed Leamington and remembers a Floodlit Cup game against Telford when Wolves legend Ron Flowers played for them. Roy Bradley signed Bob for Saltisford Rovers; Bob rates the 1970/71 Racing Club Warwick team as the best he played in. Bob had two spells with Racing Club Warwick he also played for Pottertons, AP Works on Saturdays and Leamington Southend and Whittle Wanderers on Sundays. Bob rated Dennis Farr, Ian Walker, Mick Coop, Roger Talbot and Ivor Talbot as the best players he played with or against. Music fans in Leamington and Warwick will know Bob as a talented singer. In 1997 Bob appeared on Matthew Kelly's TV show Stars in their Eyes as Bob Dylan! It was a great performance. Bob still performs with his band the Bob Phillips Rhythm Dylan Band, a huge Dylan fan his favourite song is Mr Tambourine Man.

Leamington and Warwick Sunday League XI from the 1960s and 1970s

I ran a poll on a Facebook to ask which players they would vote for in legends XI, below is the team which was voted. This team would have been competitive at a higher league, to be honest you could have picked three or four teams from the 1960s and 1970s and they all would have been very good.

Malc Hyland 17
Pep Gill 20
Roger Talbot 20
Keith Orme 26
Ian Walker 48
Chris Elliott 24
Paul Coleman 28
Ian Montgomery 36
Ivor Talbot 23
Olly Guinane 37
Dennis Farr 42

Subs

Dave Garratt Duncan Gardner Barry Whitlock Alan Stacey Roger Constable, Cliff Morby

Chapter Four – The time machine, news stories and memorable matches

A look at some random weekend fixtures in local football, which players and teams made the headlines. Over a hundred years of football history in Leamington and Warwick in News Stories. We will also down memory lane looking at some memorable matches from Lockheed Leamington, AP Leamington and Leamington FC.

The Time Machine

4th May 1951

Lockheed beat Banbury Spencer

Fred Keeble scored both goals in a 2.0 win, the first was a penalty. Hughie Morrow was pick of the Lockheed forwards.

Saltisford Rovers earn good win over Coventry Amateurs

Cliff Mancini and Jack Flaherty scored the goals in a 2.1 win, Coventry's goal was an own goal by Stradling.

11th November 1955

Warwick Town score six goals

Shaw scored three, Gillespie two and Collins completed the scoring as Warwick Town beat Bedworth Trent Valley WMC 6.1.

Warwick Town – Roystron, Jakeman, Greenhall, Bethell, Gummery, Riley, O'Farrell, Chalkley, Shaw,

Gillespie, Collins

4th April 1956

St George's win Lockheed Cup

St George's Boys club beat South Leamington Juniors 4.1 at The Windmill Ground. Rattcliffe, White, Horley and an own goal for St George's. Parsons scored for South Leamington.

31st August 1964

Lockheed try two new players

Lockheed have Colin Davies and Cyril Parry both unavailable for a Midland League game at Denaby. Two young Leamington players Brian Jenkins and Noel De Courcey are both brought in to make their debuts, Brian and Noel work at the Lockheed factory.

Lockheed - Thompson, Coleman, Lane, Jenkins, Knox, Hancock's, Ward, De Courcey, Connelly, Marriott, Hall

16th October 1967

Holmes earns Brakes a point

Heavy rain didn't help the football as Lockheed drew 1.1 at Alfreton, Ray Holmes gave The Brakes the lead but Broadhurst a former Lockheed player equalised. Brakes included new signings Alan Vest and Jack Dutchin.

3rd November 1973

Southend through thanks to Bryan

Striker Alan Bryan hit a hat rick for Leamington Southend in a 6.2 win over Radford United which put the team into the semi-final of the Warwick Advertiser Cup. John Bull got two goals and Mick Collins completed the scoring. Neville Hawtin and Mick Butler in reply for Radford.

Westlea Reserves through in cup

In a Division One cup tie Westlea Reserves beat Itchington Sports 2.1, Mick Chimes and Roger Townsend with the goals. Roger Mann scored for Itchington.

6th April 1971

Amateurs in Lockheed fifteen

Lockheed Leamington manager Geoff Coleman has named South Leamington Amateurs Billy Shanahan and Keith Jones in his fifteen man squad for a Midland League Cup semi-final against Arnold.

Lightfoot, Steane, Davis, Lawton, Shrimpton, Hall Brady, Pattison, Shanahan, Jones, Sweenie, Taylor, Whitehead, Matthews, Flanagan

14th October 1972

Westlea ten goal warning

Westlea Wanderers hammered Leamington Postal 10.1 in the Leamington League Division One internal Cup match. Dennis Woodhead scored five goals, Keith Billington two goals and one each for Ian Montgomery, Andy Townsend and Keith Gould. Nicholls got Leamington Postal's consolation goal.

Southend in comfortable win

Leamington Southend beat St Dominic's 4.1 with goals from Alan Bryan (two) John Bull and Roger Talbot. Mick McGreavey scored St Dominic's goal.

30th September 1972

Whitnash Youth grab late win

Whitnash scored late goals through Paul Carey and Mick Murphy to beat Westlea Reserves 2.1, Westlea's goal was scored by Roger Townsend.

22nd March 1969

Winsams set for the double

Winsams reach the final of the Warwick Advertiser Cup with a 3.1 win over Bishop's Itchington. Barry Whitlock, Basil Astill and George Ellard with the goals. Ron Lewin got the villagers goal.

1st October 1977

Westlea Wonders

Westlea's new striker Duncan Gardner scored two goals, Ian Montgomery and Don Grantham also scored in a 4.1 win over Avon Borough.

Comfortable win for Bishop's Itchington

Paul Skidmore, Steve Cooper and Leno Addavide all scored in a 3.0 win over Khalsa

20th December 1975

Whittle Owe it to Olly

Striker Olly Guinane scored a hat rick as Whittle Wanderers beat Wellesbourne.

Westlea hammer Leamington Southend

Westlea won 6.2 Mike Berry got a hat rick, Dennis Woodhead, Alan Holder and Ian Montgomery also scored. Roger Talbot and Noel Dillion in reply for Leamington Southend.

20th March 1971

Whittle win Division Two Cup

Guinane scored two goals; Cunningham and Condon for Whittle in a 4.1 win over Whitnash Youth. Long scored for Whitnash.

Avon Borough hit Six

David Bridges scored four as Avon beat Filton 6.0; Alan Priest also scored two goals.

28th August 1967

Veteran helps Lockheed win

Former Notts County and Derby County right half Don Roby helped Lockheed beat Loughborough United 2.1. Ray Holmes and Syd Hall on target for the Brakes

14th February 1968

Leamington Celtic score nine

Joe Brown scored five goals as Leamington Celtic beat Kineton United 9.3, Long and Burke scored two goals each. Ranklin and Gill scored for Kineton.

17th September 1977

Gardner golden goals

Duncan Gardner scored seven of Westlea Wanderers goals as they hammered Brew XI 10.0.

Leamington Southend beat Chadwick End

Norman Bass and Ivor Talbot scored the goals in a 2.1 win

14th January 1978

It's looking good for Long Itchington

Long Itchington hammered Chadwick End 5.1 goals from Barry Neal and two apiece for John Woodhouse and Bobby Hancock's. Roger Palmer scored for Chadwick End; the fine win edges Long Itchington towards the Sunday League championship.

Bishop's Itchington edge Leamington Celtic 4.3

Leon Addivide scored two goals, Don Hill and Barry Horne for Bishop's. Dennis Long, Paddy Crowley and Mick Murphy scored for Leamington Celtic.

28th January 1978

Four for Edgington

Steve Edgington scored four as B&B Trailers beat Whittle Reserves 5.1

Winner from Crowley

Paddy Crowley scored the only goal as Leamington Celtic beat Avon Borough

4th January 1968

Winsams Top century mark

Winsams gained there thirteenth win of the season and passed a century of goals as they hammered Warwick Printing 12.2. Winsams goals were scored by Whitlock, Ward, Ladyman, Parkes, Butler, Cummings and two own goals. Lewis and Thombes scored for the Printers.

Westlea beat St Mary's 9.2

Dennis Woodhead gets three goals, braces for Keith Gould, Chris Elliott and Barry Phillips.

Division One hat ricks

John Rose and Mick Chimes got hat ricks as Westlea Wanderers hammered Chadwick End 13.0. Olly Guinane scored three goals for Whittle Wanderers in a 5.2 win v Leamington Postal.

28th October 1978

A day for hat ricks

Kebby Dhesi (Khalsa) Paddy Crowley (Whittle Wanderers) Dabber Broughton (Radford United) Tony Sollis (Westlea Reserves) Bob Haines and Andy Griffin (Bulldog Sports) all scored three or more goals in an entertaining weekend local football.

15th April 1972

Tony Duggan scores four for Bubbenhall

The village team beat Armfield Rangers 5.3 in the Coventry and Central Warwickshire Premier League thanks to four from Duggan and one from Carey.

Big wins for Bishop's Itchington and Leamington Postal

Steve Cooper scored five for Bishop's and two for Leon Addivade two in a 7.1 win over Kenilworth WMC. Leamington Postal beat Harbury 8.2 four goals for Mick Clark and two for Jim Barry.

28th March 1979

Bright hope Bain lifts smart AP

Goals from youngster Roger Bain, Tom Kilkelly and an own goal as AP Leamington beat Witney 3.2. Roger a recent signing from Oadby Town was making his first full appearance.

17th April 1979

Hurst praises Gardner

England's 1966 World Cup winning hero now Telford manager Geoff Hurst praised Duncan Gardner as he scored the winner for AP Leamington. Brakes beat Telford 1.0, Hurst said Gardner is good enough for the Football League.

10th March 1975

Scriggins magic in AP rout

Dave Scriggins scored a hat rick in an entertaining 5.3 win over Dunstable Town. Mick Keeley and Adrian Stewart also scored for the Brakes. Dunstable's goals were scored by West Bromwich Albion legend Jeff Astle and future Leamington player George Cleary.

8th December 1979

Eight for Edgington

Steve Edgington scored eight for Leek Wootton in a 12.1 win over Avana Sports.

22nd April 2009

Westlea Wanderers win Birmingham County FA Vase

Westlea beat Leamington Hibernian 4.0, goals from Tom Friend, Neil Stacey, James Hardy and Luke Cole

11th May 2011

Westlea beat AC Cricketers in Vase final at Great Barr

Tom Friend got the winner against Leamington rivals Cricketers in the Birmingham County FA Vase final. It was Westlea's fourth appearance in the final since 2007 winning two and losing two.

News stories

1915

England cricketer stationed In Leamington Spa

Elias Henry "Patsy" Hendren was based at a munitions factory in Royal Leamington Spa during World War One. At the outbreak of the war

Patsy joined the 23rd (Service) Battalion of the Royal Fusiliers he remained on home service where he was posted to Leamington Spa where he worked in the lathe as a tuner.

Patsy was born in Middlesex on the 5th February 1889, at the age of sixteen he joined Lord's ground staff and in 1907 he made his first class debut for Middlesex. A prolific batsman who would play 833 times for Middlesex scoring 170 centuries averaging 50.80. An occasional bowler taking 47 wickets. Wisden cricketer of the year in 1920 he made his England test debut in the Ashes tour of 1920/21. Patsy played a total of 51 tests for his country, scoring 3,525 runs at an average of 47.63. Credited with wearing the first safety helmet against the West Indies at Lords in 1933, Patsy scored his highest total of 205 against them a few years previously.

Patsy was also a fine footballer who played as a wing forward and inside forward for Queens Park Rangers, Brentford, Manchester City and Coventry City. A famous goal for Coventry City was in an FA Cup First Round shock win over Preston North End on 15th January 1910. Patsy played thirty three times for the Bantams scoring fourteen goals. In 1911 he re-joined Brentford playing for The Bees until 1927. Patsy once played for England in an unofficial Victory International against Wales in 1919. Wales beat England 2.1 with goals from the legendary winger Billy Meredith. England also included William Ball who was with Leamington Town as a youth player.

On the 12th March 1948 it was announced that Patsy would be visiting Leamington. He would be speaking to youth leaders at the Irwin Memorial Hall in Leamington. Patsy was keen to meet sportsmen, youth leaders and youth clubs interested in sport.

When Patsy was based in Leamington he would have played cricket and football for local teams he was a fine player in both sports. Patsy's brother Dennis also played for Middlesex a second brother John was killed in 1916 whilst serving for the Royal Fusilier's. A sporting legend that became part of Leamington's history, Patsy is third on the list of all time run scorers in first class cricket behind Jack Hobbs and Frank Woolley which is indeed an impressive achievement.

3rd May 1924

Warwick Town win Birmingham Junior Cup

Warwick Town beat Chapel End 1.0 to win the cup at Highfield Road, Coventry in front of 1500 spectators. West scored the winning goal in the first half. Fred Askew would soon sign for Coventry City; he later played for Leamington Town.

Warwick Town –Aston, Patsons, Squires, Askew, Bright, R Walker, Francis, West, Harris, Carter, T Walker

24th August 1929

Leamington sign new players

Leamington Town have signed inside forward Bill Arblaster who played in the Football League for Merthyr Tydfil and Gillingham. Promising player Sidney Frank Halliday has also signed his father played for Leamington Town twenty five years ago.

22nd February 1930

Millard helps Leamington earn draw

Bert Millard who was capable of playing as a forward or centre half, helped Leamington Town draw 2.2 with Redditch. 2.0 down at half time Millard passed a clever ball to Taylor to score then Arblaster equalised. Bert had previously played for Birmingham, Coventry City, Crystal Palace and Charlton Athletic.

Leamington Town – Hyde, Holmes, Partridge, Shanks, Compton, Clarke, G Taylor, Cooper, Millard, Arblaster, W Taylor

24th August 1932

Leamington Town select four local players for opening match

Compton, Hunt, Reading and Harris are the local players; Town supporters have requested more Leamington players in the team. Cooper and Rollason are the professional players selected.

Burdett, Eustace, Coldicott, Shanks, Cooper, Compton, Hunt, Styan, Rollason, Reading, Harris

16th April 1938

Leamington St John's FC win the Foleshill Nursing Association Cup

The team from Leamington Spa beat Exhall Colliery 5.0 at the Morris Sports Ground in Courthouse Green. Two goals from Oswin, a goal each from Chaplin, Hughes and Bass completed the scoring.

Exhall Colliery – Handley, Sockett, Taylor, Hall, Rouse, Osborne, Boswell, Dixon, Keeble, Ward, Randle

Leamington St John's – Burdett, Watson, Harrison, Montgomery, Tallis, Stringer, Chaplin, Bass, Oswin, Hughes, Sauce

8th March 1940

Birmingham FC to play at Leamington

Birmingham FC is set to provisionally play three matches at The Windmill Ground against Walsall, Wolverhampton Wanderers and Coventry City. If the situation were not to change with Birmingham's home ground St Andrews some of the matches in Leamington may be played in midweek.

10th May 1985

Player makes legal history

James Condon a footballer from Leamington made legal history after winning a claim for thousands of pounds against a player who fouled him.

James suffered two compound fractures of the leg in 1980 whilst playing for Whittle Wanderers against Khalsa. The injuries caused him to take a year off work with his injuries. It set the precedence for the future a high profile case in February 1998 when a reckless tackle from Wolverhampton Wanderers player Kevin Muscat ended the career of Charlton Athletic player Matt Holmes.

5th March 1967

Jimmy Hill plays in South Leamington birthday celebration match

Coventry City manager Jimmy Hill lined up for a select-Past XI at the Windmill Ground for a match against South Leamington who were celebrating their 21st birthday. The Select-Past XI were managed by Southam man Arthur Cox who went onto have a great management career they also included Lockheed Leamington legend Bill Draper and Coventry City assistant manager Alan Dicks.

South Leamington – Tony Partridge, Terry Keen, Keith Orme, Danny Conner, Barry Ferguson, Johnny Butler, Mick Butler, George Ellard, Micky Fox, Dennis Farr, Barry Whitlock

Select-Past XI – Tony Lines, George Draper, Derek Savage, Alan Dicks, Roger Gill, Brian Jenkins, Doug Talbot, Bobby Hancock's, Noel De Courcey, Jimmy Hill, Bill Draper

South Leamington won 4.1 goals from Farr, Conner, Mick Butler and Ellard. De Courcey scored for the Select-Past XI.

From Lockheed Leamington to captain of the All Whites

Alan Vest was an experienced forward when he signed for Lockheed Leamington in 1967; he began his career with home town team Barnsley then had spells with Kings Lynn, Boston United, Spalding United and

Worksop Town. I contacted Alan on Facebook and asked him a couple of questions.

I believe that you had a spell with Lockheed Leamington in the 1960s?

I certainly did after playing for Rugby Town and it was a great club at the time and I still have great memories even though it was a long trip from Oakham to Leamington. . I live in Perth Western Australia now after having stints in New Zealand all round Australia, Singapore and Sarawak Malaysia for eight years in the 19 90s and then Perth Glory.

I believe that you also played for New Zealand at international level did you enjoy playing for the All Whites?

Yes I captained New Zealand who were coached by Barry Trueman who had been my tutor at Leicester College in the UK

Alan played seventeen times for New Zealand scoring six goals between 1972 and 1973.

Famous match

Australia   3-3 New Zealand 18th March 1973

Australia - Doug Utjesenovic 11', Ray Baartz 17', Branko Buljevic 26' -

New Zealand - Alan Vest 10', Dennis Tindall 49', Bobby Hogg 86' OG)

Australia:

Ron Corry, Doug Utjesenovic, Peter Wilson, Manfred Schaefer, Bobby Hogg, Ray Richards, Jim Mackay,   Jim Rooney, Adrian Alston, Ray Baartz, Branko Buljevic.

Coach: Rale Rasic.

New Zealand:

Kevin Curtin; Maurice Tillotson, Colin Latimour, John Staines [c], Ron Armstrong;   Brian Turner, Tommy Randles, Brian Hardman (Tony Sibley'); Alan Vest, Dennis Tindall, Dave Taylor (Max Davies)

Coach: Barrie Truman.

A World Cup qualifier between the southern hemisphere rivals finished 3.3 in Sydney, however Australia would pip the All Whites and qualify for West Germany 1974.

Match information obtained from Copyright Andre Zlotkowski and RSSSF.com 2004/15, many thanks

1st February 1975

Westlea facing shock exit from Cup

A little known rule regarding eligibility over players looks certain to lead to the expulsion of Westlea Wanderers from the Birmingham County FA Junior Sunday Cup. Ringspanners of Bromsgrove who were beaten by Westlea 2.1 in the last round complained that Westlea goalkeeper Malc Hyland shouldn't have played. Malc had previously played for Racing Club Warwick in the Birmingham Senior Amateur Cup on Saturdays. Ian Walker who scored both of Westlea's goals said that we would never have played him had we known. Westlea were expelled from the competition after the Birmingham FA investigated Ringspanners complaint.

14th November 1951

England Football team train at Lockheed ground

Prior to a Home International at Villa Park, Walter Winterbottom's team set up in Leamington Spa. The team trained on Lockheed Leamington's Windmill Ground. England's opponents Ireland also set up in the town before the match. The match itself was won by England by two goals to nil, Nat Lofthouse scored both goals. England's team included debutant goalkeeper Gil Merrick, Alf Ramsey, Billy Wright and Tom Finney.

13th February 1953

Town beat Saltisford in derby match

Warwick Town beat neighbours Saltisford Rovers 4.2 at Hampton Road their first win over Rovers for two years. Turner, Moore, Noon and an own goal for Warwick. Weston and McKeown for Rovers, Warwick included Polish player Ziggmunt playing his first game for the club.

Saltisford Rovers – Minett, Parker, Goodison, Raven, Stradling, E Mancini, King, Flaherty, Weston, McKeown, C Mancini

Warwick Town – Grimwood, Ziggmunt, Gummery, Bennett, Brindley, Turner, Collins, Henn, Moore, Noon, Combstock

11th December 1976

All Star Charity match

Gary Newbon XI v Captain Fantastic Disco XI

Sunday 12th December at AP Leamington, Tachbrook Road – admission 25p

Guest players included – Gary Newbon, Jasper Carrott, Alan Hinton and Trevor East.

Leamington Town's FA Cup run in the 1935/36 season

Leamington Town reached the 3rd qualifying round of the FA Cup beating four teams in previous rounds – Cradley Heath, Nuneaton Town, Birmingham Trams and Wellington Town before losing to Kidderminster Harriers 6.3. Leamington would have been one game away from facing Football League teams in the First Round proper. Leamington had some talented players in their team; Alfred Sabin was a right half who previously played for Birmingham City. Albert Shanks was an outside right who played once for Coventry City. Leamington's captain was George Green the towns greatest ever player, the former England international who won the FA Cup with Sheffield United in 1925 was coming to the end of his career but was still a superb player.

19th October 1935

Leamington Town 2.1 Wellington Town – FA Cup 2nd round qualifying

Goals from Eastwood and Green win the tie for Leamington

Leamington Town – Handy, Sabin, Symonds, Reading, Green, Cole, Shanks, Askew, Forrest, Eastwood, Woodward.

4th May 1962

Nine goals in benefit game for Lockheed full back

A testimonial game for long serving Lockheed full back Mick Lane attracted a 1000 supporters who were treated to nine goals. A team of All Stars beat The Brakes 7.2 with goals from Jeff Astle and Alan Withers (Notts County) Ivan Hollett (Mansfield) Don Roby (Derby) and Peter Denton (Coventry City). Lockheed scored through Lane and an Astle own goal. Lockheed manager Syd Ottewell used his East Midlands connections well to attract some good players for this match; Jeff Astle would later play for West Bromwich Albion and England.

15th November 1969

Saltisford youngster has trial with Leicester City

Sixteen year old Steve Cooper has gone on trial at Second Division Leicester City; Steve scored three goals on his Saltisford debut three weeks ago. Saltisford manager Roy Bradley said Steve had speed, height, ball control and keenness to make the grade. Spotted playing for Bishop's Itchington, Coventry City and Wolves also made enquiries about him. Steve got his hat rick as Saltisford Rovers hammered Darlaston Reserves 8.1 on November 1st. Martin Baldwin also got three, one apiece for Mac Evans and John Condon.

8th July 1972

Lockheed Leamington sign two players

Manager Geoff Coleman has signed two players from Corby Town, Dennis Walker and Steve Sherry. Dennis previously played for West Ham United's youth and reserve teams. In the mid to late 1960s Dennis played with Frank Lampard Snr, Trevor Brooking and Harry Redknapp for The Hammers. Dennis also played for Luton Town the same time Bruce Rioch was at the club. Steve is a Scot who was previously with Albion Rovers and Huddersfield Town.

16th December 1927

Leamington's sixth successive away win

Leamington beat Nuneaton two nil thanks to two second half goals from Gregory. The Magpies sixth away win after previously beating Hereford, Bourneville, Rugby, Walsall Reserves and Evesham. If Leamington's home form was better they would have been top of the league. Joe McClure had a solid match against Nuneaton he would soon go onto greater things playing for Everton with the legendary Dixie Dean.

Leamington Town – Edgington, Holmes, Partridge, Morris, McClure, Homer, Hunt, Shanks, Gregory,

Wilson, Compton

23rd January 1937

Lockheed score eight goals

Lockheed beat Rover Sports 8.0 thanks to goals from Griffin who scored four, A Saywell two and one each for N Saywell and Croft.

Lockheed – Heath, Bayliss, Thacker, Sabin, Blackburn, Loos, Ledwith, A Saywell, N Saywell, Griffin, Croft

29th September 1923

Leamington Town win at Tamworth

Leamington beat Tamworth 3.1 thanks to goals from two goals from Saunders where Rowlatt was involved with both goals, Blakemore added a third goal.

Leamington Town – Horsley, Holmes, Glaze, Guest, Fleming, Boxley, Rowlatt, Blakemore, Saunders,

Brittle, Key

15th May 1920

Leamington St John's beat Spa rivals for cup

Leamington St John's beat Leamington Town 4.1 to win the Birmingham Junior Cup at Highfield Road the home of Coventry City. Williams scored twice, Hollis and Knight also scored. Reynolds scored Town's goal.

Leamington Town – Allcock, Reading, Jonas, Chockley, Green, Frost, Steane, Bull, Rowlatt, Reynolds, Barber

Leamington St John's – Reading, Hughes, Cash, Mason, Tallis, Pountney, Knight, Thayers, Hollis, Williams, Hallard

6th May 1921

Leamington Town win the Birmingham Junior Cup

Leamington Town win the cup to add to the championship of the Coventry and North Warwickshire League. Leamington Town beat Lower Gornal 5.0 at Manor Park, Nuneaton; Holders of the cup were town rivals Leamington St John's. Two goals each for Rowlatt and Gumbley, one for Key. Leamington Town included a young George Green who would go onto play for Sheffield United and England.

Leamington Town – Alcock, Gumbley, Jonas, Green, Evans, Checkley, Deeming, Rowlatt, Walker, Key

20th July 1933

Leslie Bruton joins Leamington Town

Leslie who was centre forward for Liverpool last season made a surprise move to Leamington. A player with experience in England and Scotland with Southampton, Blackburn Rovers and Raith Rovers. Leslie was born in Foleshill, Coventry he would become captain of Leamington Town.

In November 1933 Leslie scored in a 3.1 win over Hinckley, Metherill scored two goals.

Leamington Town – Green, Cole, Symonds, Shanks, Bunn, Sabin, Askew, Bruton, Cooper, Eastwood, Metherill

January 1934 Leslie scored twice in a 5.1 win over Birmingham Trams, Askew, Cooper and Eastwood also scored.

Leamington Town – Green, Trew, Symonds, Shanks, Bunn, Sabin, Askew, Bruton, Cooper, Eastwood, Ensor

In December 1934 he joined Hinckley and in July 1935 Leslie joined Coventry City as assistant trainer. The Bantams must have regretted not signing Leslie when he was younger; he began his football career with local team Bell Green Wesleyans.

20th May 1954

Tracey Thomas becomes honorary secretary of Lockheed Leamington

Twenty Six year old Tracey succeeds Arthur Hunt who was associated with the club for sixteen years. Tracey would later become secretary of Leamington Sunday League and be involved with local football for over fifty years. Sadly Tracey passed away in March 2017 a true stalwart of Leamington football.

24th September 1955

Warwickshire bowler joins Lockheed

Lockheed have signed Warwickshire bowler Ray Carter who had been playing centre half for the reserves. Ray was introduced to the club by Fred Gardner who coaches the reserves.

Ray made his first team debut for Lockheed in March 1956 against Walsall Reserves. The team lined up as follows – Thornton,Allen,Hawker,Sloan,Carter,Brazier,Brison,Grimwood,Bayliss,Morrow,Burrows

7th September 1956

Lockheed Cobblers connection

At the beginning of the 1956/57 season, Division Three South team Northampton Town had a few Lockheed Leamington connections. 1950s Brakes legends Bill Draper and Hugh Morrow were at Northampton along with Charlie Dutton. Charlie joined Lockheed on loan from Northampton in January 1957; he previously played for Coventry City. Charlie was a popular player at Highfield Road scoring nine goals in twenty eight appearances; he joined The Bantams in 1952 from Derby County a reserve player with The Rams. After leaving Lockheed, Charlie played for Rugby, Hinckley, Bedworth and Brereton Social.

The other Lockheed connection was a young full back called Geoff Coleman, he was keeping the experienced Ron Patterson in the second team. Geoff made his Cobblers debut the previous season against Queens Park Rangers, A Bedworth kid who played previously for Banbury Spencer and Bedworth Town. In October 1959 Lockheed Leamington signed twenty three year old Geoff from Northampton Town. The Cobblers had a new policy that all professionals should become full timers. Geoff had a job outside football and could not agree to the new scheme so Brakes manager Les Latham stepped into sign him. Geoff would become one of the clubs finest full backs playing in the great Brakes team of the early to mid-1960s under Syd Ottewell. In May 1965 he joined Redditch linking up with former Lockheed teammates Noel De Courcey and Brian and Roy Bradley. In the late 1960s Geoff also played for Rugby Town and a second spell with Redditch. Towards the end of his career Geoff played at centre half, in March 1969 he was appointed manager of Lockheed Leamington. Geoff was thirty two when he was appointed as Lockheed manager and still playing for Redditch, chairman Jack Rogers said that he was the man most likely to bring success to the club and had contacts to bring more local players into the side. In his early days as manager Geoff was assisted in training by Syd Hall and Jim Watson. One of Geoff's best signings was Dennis Taylor who would become a loyal and great player for Lockheed/AP Leamington. Geoff also managed Nuneaton Borough, Wealdstone and VS Rugby in the 1970s.

23rd August 1958

Too many old heads say Lockheed fans!

Lockheed Leamington have signed twenty one professional's in a bid for success, some fans have said that the players are too old but Brakes manager Les Latham has said they are still top class footballers. The calibre of players Lockheed signed were first class, George Lee a former West Bromwich Albion winger and ex Coventry City players Charlie Timms and Jimmy Hill.

One young player signed would be inspiring a twenty year old winger called Ernie Ward who was on Coventry City's books. Ernie would become one of Lockheed's star players of the 1960s.

Lockheed Leamington squad August 1958

Goalkeepers – Lawler, Lines, Jackson

Half backs –
Hancocks,Knight,Dougall,Hawker,Norden,Ward,Woodhouse,Hoare,Hadlum,Mountford,Walters,Fenn,

Wright, Keen

Full backs –Bennett, Lane, Timmins, Draper, Savage

Forwards –
Hawkins,Evans,Robertson,Clark,Waite,White,Whetton,Long,Hill,Lee,Ward,Pearson,Horley,Molloy,

Hopkins, Wiles

31st October 1959

Ken Brown signs for Lockheed

Brakes manager Les Latham has signed Ken to play outside left. Recently with Hinckley, Coventry kid Ken has also spent time with Coventry City, Nottingham Forest and Torquay United.

6th May 1967

Brian Daykin new Bourne Town manager

Lockheed Leamington full back Brian Daykin has been named player manager of Bourne Town. The twenty nine year old who has played for Derby County and Notts County has also spent time in Australia.

9th October 1967

Wolverhampton Wanderers legend hammered by Lockheed

Eddie Clamp the former Wolves and England defender was unable to prevent his team Lower Gornal getting a thrashing by Lockheed. The Brakes won 8.2 in this one sided Birmingham Senior Cup match. Frans Derko, Syd Hall and Bill Atkinson with two goals each. Peter Lawton and Ray Holmes also got a goal each. Frans Derko was signed from Mansfield Town; the Italian inside forward played one game for Mansfield. Frans scored a few goals for Lockheed in the 1967/68 season.

23rd July 1976

FA Cup hero joins AP Leamington

Young striker Stuart Gallagher has joined AP Leamington on trial. Stuart was Coventry Sporting's two goal hero as they beat Division Four Tranmere Rovers in the FA Cup First Round.

Stuart's first team chances were limited due to first choice strikers Adrian Stewart and Mick Keeley. Tom Starkey joined AP Leamington in 1979, Tom played with Stuart in the Cup shock against Tranmere.

Memorable Leamington Charity Cup finals

11th May 1951

Brico 4.1 South Leamington

Coventry side Brico beat a young South Leamington team at The Windmill. Burnell scored for South Leamington, Talbot missed a great chance but Brico going three up in the first half gave them a good cushion.

2nd May 1962

Lockheed Leamington 0.2 Coventry City

Coventry beat Lockheed 2.0 in the final, Scottish international Stewart Imlach scored both goals. Coventry City manager Jimmy Hill played himself at outside right, Ron Farmer, Dietmar Bruck and Colin Holder also played.

3rd August 1974

The Fergie Connection

In the summer of 1974 Nuneaton Borough visited Scotland in pre-season. Their first match was against East Stirlingshire, this match would be significant as it was a certain Alex Ferguson's first match as a manager. Nuneaton Borough had a few Leamington and Warwick connections, Borough manager at the time was Geoff Coleman. Geoff was a full back for Lockheed Leamington and later manager in the 1960s. The match itself was a comfortable three nil win for Nuneaton Borough with future AP Leamington strikers Bob Turpie and Bobby Vincent with the goals. Alex Ferguson had just finished playing and this would be his first managerial position. As they say the rest is history he would go on to become one of the greatest managers of all time. Alex was assisted at Aberdeen and Manchester United by Archie Knox brother of Leamington legend Jimmy Knox.

Former Coventry City full back and future Racing Club Warwick and AP Leamington manager Dietmar Bruck also played in this match. Dennis Oakes's father Jack Oakes played for Lockheed Leamington, Dennis also played cricket for Warwickshire. Future AP Leamington players Tom Starkey, Ian Goodwin, Steve Briscoe and Alan Jones were also in Nuneaton Borough's squad.

Ian Goodwin briefly played with Alex Ferguson at Falkirk this would have been about 1969. Ian remembers the East Stirling game well, I asked him about his time in Scotland" I spent a month at Falkirk on trial and trained and played with Alex every day. Things didn't work out and within months l had joined Coventry City" Ian played for Leamington in the 1984/85 season in his younger days he played against some great strikers – John Charles, Derek Dougan, Alan Gilzean, Mick Channon, Ted McDougall. The best striker at non-league level? "I would say was a guy called George Duck who played for Wealdstone. He could have graced the game at a much higher level but chose to work as a sports master and play non-league."

Nuneaton Borough: Knight, Stephens, Bruck, Oakes, Goodwin, Baxter, Starkey, Turpie, Owen, Lewis, Vincent. Subs: Jones, Briscoe and Newton.

12th March 1976

Brian Hill joins Racing Club Warwick

New Racing Club Warwick manager Gerry Baker has signed former Coventry City teammate Brian Hill. Gerry has also named local amateurs

Alan Wilkes and Stuart Walker in the squad to face Coleshill. Defender Kenny Sanders has left to join Syd Hall at VS Rugby.

Racing Club Warwick – Hyland, McGuff, Taylor, Clarke, Cooper, Lane, Shrimpton, Warom, Wilkes, Walker, Hill, Allsop, Morby, Barraclough

Brian didn't stay long at Hampton Road, in August 1976 aged thirty five he announced his retirement due to injuries. Brian was born in Bedworth on 31st July 1941 he began his career at Coventry City as an apprentice. On 30th April 1958 Brian became youngest ever debutant and goal scorer at 16 years 273 days in a Division Three (South) match against Gillingham. Brian played for Coventry City until 1971 making 246 appearances, in his time at Highfield Road he played in five divisions for the Sky Blues. Brian was an excellent defensive player and man marker, he was a versatile defender. Towards the end of his career he played for Bristol City, Torquay United and hometown team Bedworth United.

It is a shame injuries restricted him at Racing Club Warwick as he would have been a great player to be in the squad. Sadly Brian passed away on 27th October 2016.

4th June 1988

AP Leamington stars play against England

In June 1988 former AP Leamington players Tim Garner and Cliff Campbell were playing for Aylesbury United. The Ducks had just won the Southern Premier Division (Beazer Homes League) gaining promotion to the GM Vauxhall Conference. Bobby Robson's England team were looking forward to the European Championships in West Germany. On the 4th of June 1988 England played a unique pre-tournament friendly against Aylesbury United. Journalist Frank McGhee a friend of Aylesbury chairman Charlie Doherty had come up with the idea of England playing a non-league team. The idea was based on Hungary's great team of the 1950s who would often play local teams before major matches. England sent a full squad to Buckingham Road and predictably it was a comfortable win for the national team. Peter Beardsley was England's man of the match with four goals. Trevor Steven, Gary Lineker and Dave Watson also scored. Aylesbury goal machine Cliff Hercules however did go very close to scoring with a header. It would be Cliff Campbell's last match before retiring to take up a coaching position. Aylesbury managed by Trevor Gould the former Coventry City player would spend one year in the higher division. England that summer would have a dismal tournament losing every match.

For one match a couple of Brakes heroes got the chance to play against some world class players, not bad opposition to finish with Cliff.

2nd January 1999

England International and European Cup winner plays for Stratford Town

At the age of forty five former Aston Villa winger Tony Morley played for Interlink Express Midland Alliance side Stratford Town.

Marcus Hamill

I contacted Marcus Hamill via Facebook; Marcus was a few years older than me at school. He was destined to be a footballer he was a very talented midfielder. Marcus played with Tony at Stratford Town in 1999.

I believe that you played with Tony Morley at Stratford?

Yes Tony Morley was a true professional and a great character also Andy Blair did a season helping with coaching back in the day.

Could you tell me about how you got into football and what teams you played for?

I was at Stratford Town for five years and also a spell at Evesham during that time. I grew up playing as a kid for Christ the King FC .I was scouted by Stoke City at the age of twelve I then spent time up in Stoke –on-Trent staying in digs. Mick Mills was first team manager and Sammy Chung was physio. I trained with Aaron Callaghan and various other professionals. I spent three years back and forth to Stoke but not as often as they would have liked me as my parents didn't drive.

At the age of sixteen unfortunately I didn't get signed as they said my height had not improved in the time I was with them. During three years at Stoke I also failed England trials at Loughborough again was told I was too small!

Heart broken and deflated! I then moved about playing for Masseys, CTK, Highway and Coundon FC. Until being picked up for Stratford town .After Stratford I then returned to the Coventry leagues. I'm still trying now at jaguar over 35's.lol I also played for Coventry Marconi and Peugeot.

Marcus also told me that his manager at Stratford Town Len Derby was his best ever manager.

Thanks for your time Marcus

4th April 1987

Leamington lad making name for himself in USA

Paul Dougherty was born in Leamington on 12th May 1966. A midfielder/forward, Paul aged seventeen broke into Wolverhampton Wanderers first team in the 1983/84 season. Wolves at the time had a few Warwickshire connections – Graham Rodger, Tim Flowers and Mark Buckland ex AP Leamington. Paul played for Wolves when the club suffered successive relegations and ended up in the old Fourth Division. At the end of the 1986/87 season Paul joined US indoor soccer team San Diego Sockers managed by Englishman Ron Newman. Paul who is 5feet 2 excelled in the indoor game, a team mate was Polish star Kaz Deyna. Paul also played for English teams Torquay United and Cheltenham Town, but spent most of his career in the USA. Now aged fifty three Paul is currently coach of San Diego WFC SeaLions.

Memorable Matches Lockheed, AP and Leamington FC

6th September 1947

Lockheed Leamington 9.0 Oakham -Central Amateur League

Lockheed scored six goals in the second half to hammer Oakham. Four goals from Montgomery, two each for Drummond and Straddling, one goal for Pettifer.

Lockheed Leamington – Isaacson, Murphy, Smith, Stradling, Underhill, Greenwood, Drummond, Montgomery, Pettifer, Fell, Eden

1st December 1951

Lockheed Leamington 5.1 Sutton Town – Birmingham Combination

Frank Grimwood scored all five goals as Lockheed won comfortably, George scored for Sutton.

Lockheed Leamington –
Brant,Dobbs,Tooze,Hawker,Snape,Baldwin,Atkins,Grimwood,Soden,Gardner,French

Sutton Town –
Alderwich,Riley,Hobbins,Lander,Rigby,Shaw,Smith,Williams,George,Puffrey,Roberts

11th January 1958

Lockheed Leamington 3.1 Rugby Town

George Dean scored two goals for Lockheed and left back Lane also scored as they beat their Warwickshire rivals, Roberts scored for Rugby.

Lockheed Leamington –
Partridge,Jones,Lane,Hancocks,Hawker,Hawkins,Dean,Dougall,Evans,Hackett,Burrows

Rugby Town –

McCormack,Brown,Hargreaves,Brews,Livie,Gilbert,Roberts,Duggins,Awde,Mason,Kelly

15th December 1962

Sutton Town 1.6 Lockheed Leamington – West Midlands League

The Brakes earned a fine away win, thanks to two goals from Shorthose and one each for Jepson, Ward, Hall and Brian Bradley. Upton scored Sutton's consolation goal.

Sutton Town –

Johnson,Yates,Hall,Burton,Toussaint,Deebank,Upton,Bates,Wiggan,Hynett,Jones

Lockheed Leamington – Woodward, Coleman, Lane, Hancocks, B Bradley, R Bradley, Ward, Newberry, Jepson, Shorthose, Hall

30th May 1963

Lockheed Leamington 1.2 Stratford Town – Birmingham Senior Cup Final

Lockheed lost to neighbours Stratford at Moor Green's ground in Birmingham. Stratford's heroes were Sid Keenan who scored both goals and Captain Bill Rowley who gave little away to Barry Jepson. The Brakes were missing Barrie Shorthose but still expected to win, Peter Newberry scored for Lockheed.

Lockheed Leamington – Woodward, Coleman, Lane, Hancock, R Bradley, Jenkins, B Bradley, Ward,

Newberry, Jepson, Hall

Stratford Town - Stowe, Reece, Gerry, Merrett, Rowley, Gardner, Keenan, Hillman, Bent, Jessop, Morris

18th October 1965

Darlaston 2.9 Lockheed Leamington

Ray Holmes scored a sensational six goals as Lockheed hammered Darlaston. Shorthose also scored two goals and Knox completed the scoring.

Lockheed Leamington –
Crosby,Lockton,Hancocks,Haines,Knox,Jones,Parry,Ward,Holmes,Shorthose,Hall

27th November 1965

Alfreton Town 1.2 Lockheed Leamington – Midland League

Barrie Shorthouse and Ernie Ward scored the goals in a good away win for Lockheed. Whittaker scored for the home team.

Alfreton Town – Mycroft, Newton, White, Howarth, Kelsey, Morris, Whittaker, Graham, Drury, Harrison, Jepson

Lockheed Leamington –
Bayton,Lockton,Hinde,Davis,Connelly,Jones,Parry,Knox,Holmes,Shorthose,Ward

26th March 1966

Lincoln Reserves 1.2 Lockheed Leamington – Midland League

A Syd Hall penalty and a goal from Barry Shorthose secured the win for The Brakes.

Lincoln Reserves – Jeavons, Woodthorne, Pilgrim, Larkin, Heward, Farrall.Whittle, Holmes, Wells, Farmer, Hawbrook

Lockheed Leamington –
Crosby,Lockton,Hancocks,Knox,Haines,Jones,Ward,Shorthose,Holmes,Wilson,Hall

5th November 1977

Boston United 1.2 AP Leamington – FA Cup

Battling AP earn a place in the FA Cup First round proper thanks to goals from Brown and Morton. The Brakes had to come from behind as Adamson had given the home side the lead.

Boston United – Stewart, Adamson, Towie, Poplar, Phelan, Thompson, Mosker, Symm, Brown, Kabia, Callery

AP Leamington – O'Keefe, Kavanagh, Capewell, Jones, Brown, Boot, Morton, Taylor, Stewart, Keeley, Gorman

26th December 1980

AP Leamington 5.0 Telford United - Alliance Premier League

A Boxing Day classic at The Old Windmill, It was a happy first home game for AP Manager John Farrington. Telford United was managed by England World Cup winning legend Gordon Banks. The Brakes goal scorers were Micky Taylor, John Farrington, Gary Brown, Doug Hickton and Alan Jones from the penalty spot.

AP Leamington – Dulleston, Cooper, Montgomery, Jones, Brown, Ashenden, Farrington, Gorman,

Hickton (D Taylor) Gardner, M Taylor

9th November 1982

AP Leamington 5.1 Oldbury - Southern League Premier

Super striker Kim Casey scored five goals as AP thrashed Oldbury; Kim's goals were assisted by Buckland, Griffin and Campbell. Sabin replied for Oldbury, The Brakes had one of their best ever seasons winning the Southern League title.

AP Leamington – Livsey, Buckland, Britton, Rigby, Kavanagh, Woodall, MacKenzie, Casey, Griffin,

Campbell, Wilson

4th November 1986

VS Rugby 0.1 Leamington – FA Trophy

After a 1.1 draw in the first match, The Brakes won the replay at Butlin Road thanks to a first half goal from Albert Johnson. This result brought a bit of cheer to Leamington fans who had suffered for a few years. VS Rugby were a decent outfit back then with players like striker Steve Norris but Leamington had some good experienced players like Lol Chamberlain and Paul Coleman.

Leamington – Chamberlain, Williams, Upton, Rennie, Thomas, Taylor, Coleman, Trickett, Mumford, Johnson, Bushall

31st October 1987

Leamington 5.2 Bloxwich AFC - Midland Combination Premier Division

In what would be Leamington's last ever season at The Old Windmill; The Brakes got a fine win thanks to two goals from Duncan Gardner and one each for Steve Sykes, Tony Hathaway, Billy Jawanda. Duncan Gardner and Steve Montgomery brought welcome experience to this team.

Leamington - Harnett, Myton (Fitzpatrick), Philpott, Gow, Jawandha, singleton, Gardner, Sykes, Hathaway,

Montgomery, Graham.

19th August 2000

Leamington 3.1 Enville Athletic – Midland Combination Division Two

A dream start in Leamington's first ever match at the New Windmill, Josh Blake scored two goals and Nicholas Mort completed the scoring. For the 800 fans that were there that day and the dedicated people who helped make the dream happen, this match will always be a very special memory.

Leamington Paul O'Keeffe; Kevin Ariss, Simon Gulliver (Tim Romback),

Adam Ball, Liam McGovern, Will Payne, Nicholas Mort, Ian Billington (Robin Morey), Josh Blake, Mark Simmonds (Capt.), Simon Wickson (Jonny Burgess)

1st December 2001

Holly Lane 1.8 Leamington - Midland Combination Division One

Neale Perry got a hat rick; two each for Kev Ariss and Baz Shearsby, Glenn Webb completed the scoring in this fine away win.

Leamington: Richard Morris, Kevin Ariss (David Care), Will Payne, Liam McGovern, Tom Sidwell (Andrew Dix), Nick Mort (Harj Dhesi), Darren Timms, Glen Webb, Neale Perry, Barry Shearsby, Steve Thompson

26th August 2002

Leamington 5.0 Southam United - Midland Combination Premier division

Brakes earned a comfortable win over neighbours Southam thanks to two goals from Glenn Webb, one each for Jag Bahi, Josh Blake and Paul Nicholls.

Leamington: Myles Day, Jag Bahi, Simon Walker, Mark Rowland, Tom Sidwell, Darren Timms (Chris Hammond), Glen Webb, Barry Shearsby (Chris Hanrahan), Josh Blake (Brian Agar), Paul Nicholls, Steve Thompson [Capt.]

3rd April 2007

Leamington 3.1 Atherstone Town - Midland Alliance League Cup Semi Final first leg

Former Coventry City midfielder Avun Jephcott scored a hat rick as the Brakes beat Warwickshire rivals Atherstone.

Leamington Richard Morris; Jamie Towers; Martin Hier; Adam Cooper; Andy Gregory; Craig Dutton [Capt.]; Stuart Herlihy; Jon Adams (Pearson); Martin Thompson (Mackey); Avun Jephcott; James Husband (James

Atherstone Town Richard Williams; Stefan Beale (Williams); Cameron Stuart; Jamie Hood; Leigh Everitt [Capt.]; Gary Redgate; Chris Long; Ashley Wells; Chris Partridge (Gaunt); Roy Dunkley (Swan); Tommy Browett

22nd March 2008

Leamington 3.0 Bedworth United - British Gas Business Southern League Midland Division.

Liam Reynolds, Josh Blake and Guy Sanders scored second half goals as The Brakes beat Bedworth.

Leamington: Morris, Towers, Parisi, Sanders, Hier, Herlihy (Reynolds), Hadland, Husband, Marsden (Parkinson,), Blake, Jackson.
Bedworth United: Kemp, Lazarus, Jephcott, Pitham, Thackeray, Verna, Spacey (Baker, Fox), Twigger, Kinder, Simeon Williams, Jamie Williams.

23rd October 2010

Leamington 3.2 Truro City – Zamaretto League Premier Division

A goal from Rich Batchelor, an own goal and a Lewis penalty win it for The Brakes.

Leamington –
Breeden,Lycett,Morley,Downes,Sanders,Daly,Jackson,Husband,Lewis(Faulds)Wilding(Rowe)Batchelor

29th September 2015

Leamington 3.0 Slough Town -Evostik Southern League Premier Division

Two goals from Jack Edwards and a goal from Ben Mackey gave Leamington the points.

Leamington: Tony Breeden , Ben George, Connor Gudger, Joe Magunda, Jamie Hood, James Mace, Lee Moore, Richard Taundry (Ross Oulton), Ben Mackey (Wil Green), Jack Edwards (James Fry), Lee Chilton.

Slough Town: Mark Scott, Sean Fraser, Jai Dhillon, Guy Hollis, Dan Hicks, Adrian Sear , Ryan Hope, Adam Martin, Scott Harris, Lewis Putman, Warren Harris.

Chapter Five – Suburbs and surrounding villages

A look at some of the football teams from Leamington Spa's suburbs and nearby villages.

Radford United

Nev Hawtin

A Radford lad, Nev was a striker for Radford United for many years both Saturday and Sunday. Nev also played for Southam United, Cubbington Albion and Winsams. His finest match was when he scored five goals for Radford United in a 10.1 thrashing of Whittle Wanderers. I messaged Nev on Facebook and he told me "when I moved to Devon somebody knew I had played a lot and played for Paignton Villa till I was forty eight winning three trophies and then played in the friendly league till I hung my boots up at fifty six"

Teammates at Radford United included Mark Titterton, Paddy Crowley John Rawlings, Geoff Dean, Eric Talbot and Mick Butler. Mark's son Morton played for Racing Club Warwick and Leamington, Sadly both Geoff and Mick have passed away.

Thanks for your time Nev

Nev in the news

22nd March 1969

Radford score nine

Radford hammered neighbours Offchurch Nine nil in Division Three, Sewell with three. Hawtin, England and Priday with two goals each.

12th February 1977

Win for Radford United

Radford United beat Rail Wanderers 2.0 with Nev Hawtin and John Rawlings with the goals.

8th December 1979

Hat rick for Nev

Nev Hawtin scored three goals as Radford beat Whitnash 4.1 in the Division One Cup.

Radford Albion now represents the village of Radford Semele in Division Two of Tracey Thomas Leamington and District Sunday League. Albion are looking to gain promotion this season to Division One.

Whitnash

Whitnash had two good teams in the late 1960s and early 1970s, Whitnash Youth and Whitnash Warriors.

Graham Timms

Graham was a goalkeeper for Whitnash Youth FC in the 1960s and 1970s; I asked him a few questions about his career. I was keen to make contact with Graham he is a member of a Facebook group which shares memories of football in Leamington and Warwick.

Hi Graham what teams did you play for?

Whitnash Youth FC (my father's team) Lillington Sports. Warwick West End. Stretton Athletic. Southam United and Bulldog Sports.

Which players stood out in your time at Whitnash Youth?

In my father's team Whitnash Youth FC there was so many at different times. Best defenders -Chris Read. Roger Constable. Roger Brierley. Best midfielders - Chris Lea. Ian Claridge. Don Hill. Best forwards. Dennis Long. Ronnie Young. Ivor Talbot. I always rated Olly Guinane; he played for us and other teams. Olly is a good friend and a real character. Tony Partridge was probably the best goalkeeper around in my playing days.

Who are your favourite players from that era in local football?

When I played for Southam United in the Coventry & North Warwickshire League, Roger Greenaway was top class; also Brian Smith was a good player.

Graham also told me that when he was fifteen he went on a coaching course with Dennis Woodhead, they played for Leamington Boys Club. Top coaches were in attendance including Pat Whelton who was Keith Burkinshaw's assistant at Tottenham Hotspur.

Thanks for you for sharing your memories Graham

25th April 1967

Whitnash Warriors win Shield

Whitnash Warriors beat Warwick Juniors 3.2 in the Mid-Warwickshire Youth League's Thornton Walker Shield final. Warrior's goals were scored by Maurice Whittle, Paul Smith and John Bull. Ian Claridge and Ronnie Young scored for Warwick Juniors.

Whitnash Warriors also won the Lockheed Cup in May 1967, runners up in the Courier Cup. Team manager Mr White said that it has been a remarkable first season.

Whitnash Charity Cup

A competition which goes back to 1910 the first final between Whitnash and Spencer Street all proceeds distributed to the poor in the village. As the years went by teams from Coventry and Kenilworth entered in the 1912 final Coventry Humber beat Budbrooke 2.0

10th April 1920

Warwick West End win Cup

A one nil win over Kenilworth Abbey Hill secured the cup for the Warwick team. Tandy scored the goal on eighty minutes.

17th April 1933

Cubbington Albion v Flavels

Cubbington beat Flavels 3.1 with goals from Barratt, Chamberlain, Thompson. Aitken with the goal for Flavels.

2nd April 1934

Cubbington Albion v Flavels

Cubbington won 2.0 thanks to first half goals from Montgomery and Hughes, playing conditions weren't ideal high winds interfered with play. Cubbington's goals were well worked.

18th April 1938

Leamington Southend v Saltisford Rovers

Southend beat Rovers 3.2 with goals from Rogers, Letts and Croft. Gardner scored twice for Rovers.

8th April 1947

Lockheed Leamington v Saltisford Rovers

Dave Montgomery scored first for Lockheed then Frank Montgomery equalised for Saltisford. Round got the winning goal for Lockheed in extra time.

2nd April 1948

Lockheed Leamington v Saltisford Rovers

Smith gave Rovers the lead, Gardner and Drummond goals put Lockheed ahead then Frank Montgomery equalised for Rovers. Eden got the winning goal for Lockheed. David Montgomery Lockheed's centre forward the younger brother of Frank scored three goals the day before when Lockheed beat Standard Athletic 3.1 to win the Foleshill Charity Cup.

Modern era

11th May 1979

Dutch team to play Whitnash

The village team are host to ZRC Amsterdam an amateur team. They will be playing a charity match in which the proceeds will go to elderly in the village. A member of the Dutch team is married to a Warwickshire woman who helped organise the match.

Ian Shurvinton

Ian was manager of Whitnash FC from 1985 to 1992; it was a great time for the club. Ian led the team to two promotions and a championship.

1985/86 – Whitnash finished fifth in the Suburban Division Three, they gave a few teams a good hammering but lost heavily themselves which cost the team promotion.

1986/87 – Promotion is achieved! Whitnash finished second to City Supporters only by one point.

1987/88 –Consolidation as Whitnash finish mid table in the higher division.

1988/89 - A fantastic season for Whitnash, they won the Suburban Division Two title with thirty three points undefeated all season. Fifteen wins and scoring sixty two goals finishing eight points ahead of nearest rivals Brico. Whitnash also won the League Cup, a memorable double.

1989/90 – A very respectable third place finish in the Suburban Division One.

1990/91 – Leagues were merged and Whitnash competed in the Alliance Division Two, another excellent third place in the new league.

Dave Partridge was top scorer during Ian's time as manager with sixty one goals followed by Jimmy Crawford with fifty five. Other notable players were John Woodhouse, John Eales, Brendan Fraser, Martin Watkin, brothers Chris, Eddie and Willie Fitzpatrick and many more in this great Ian Shurvinton era for Whitnash FC.

Many thanks for sharing this information with me Ian; you should be very proud about your time as manager.

Hodcarrier FC

The Hodcarrier Pub in Coppice Road Whitnash was opened in 1983 by World Snooker champion Steve Davis. In the early 2000s Hodcarrier FC assembled an impressive team of local players who played for Racing Club Warwick or Leamington. Under the management of professional goalkeeper and Leamington man Jason Pearcey, they won plenty of trophies.

In 2001 they had their finest hour beating Coventry side Pilot 3.0 in the Birmingham Sunday Vase final.

Hodcarrier FC - Paul O'Keeffe , Brendan Fraser , Owen Lovelock, Harj Dhesi ,Darren Howson ,Stuart Hepburn ,Andy Lovelock, Vernor Sleem, Sniffer Eden, Steve Thompson, Richard Follett

Manager - Jason Pearcey

Stuart Hepburn

I contacted Stuart Hepburn via email and asked him a few questions about his playing career. Stuart played twenty eight times for Leamington between 2000 and 2001. Stuart also played for Racing Club Warwick in the late 1990s.

Could you tell me a bit about your junior career which teams you played for before joining Racing Club Warwick?

I started playing football as a kid for AP Juniors, playing from the age of nine with my good friend Paul Eden (Sniffer). We were really successful, Sniffer was a prolific goal scorer (how he got his nickname). This team became Whitnash Hardware FC, sponsored by Keith who ran the hardware shop on Acre Close in Whitnash. (I have a picture of the team somewhere). The success continued all the way to the Under 16's age group, at the point where we all started seeking experience in the men's league. I was also lucky to play for Warwickshire County in my teens and enjoyed trips overseas to America and France representing them. I played with a lot of the lads who would end up playing against or with at Southam, Racing Club Warwick and Leamington.

What are your memories of Hodcarrier FC and the Birmingham Vase run and final I believe that you scored in the final?

In our late teams most of the team began playing for Radford Newbold sponsored by the Newbold Comyn Arms, this then evolved into RN Hodcarrier, which ended up being The Hodcarrier FC. My father and my brother ran the Hodcarrier so the sponsorship was relatively easy to secure! It is fair to say that as The Hodcarrier we dominated the local scene for a good period of time, winning seven Cancer Cups in a row being the best example. The Birmingham Vase final win was really the pinnacle of our time. It was a combination of our strong team spirit, mix of great player and professional approach to the game that meant we had Pilot beaten before the whistle had blown the start of the game. I didn't score many in my time, but can definitely say that was the best and most satisfying goal I ever scored. I was very lucky to pick up lots of cups in my time as a football captain, but that was by far the best. We left the game and had one hell of a party back at The Hodcarrier.

There must have been a real buzz when you joined The Brakes in 2000, it must have helped that you played with Brian Agar, Paul Eden before? Cadzy was at Racing Club Warwick too.

The early days of the Brakes were amazing, as it really was a collection of the best local players, particularly from The Hodcarrier and Westlea Wanderers. One of Cadzy's biggest challenges was asking not to also play on a Sunday! It felt great to be playing there at the revival of the team; the atmosphere on the pitch was inspiring as was the support from the sidelines. I'm not sure that will be repeated again?

24th April 2014

Whitnash Town Win Coventry Charity Cup

Whitnash Town beat The Bell/AEI Rugby 3.0 at the Ricoh Arena to win the Coventry Charity Cup, two goals from Henry Leaver and one from Josh Cole won it for Town. Whitnash included Neil Stacey, Glenn Webb and Lee Scott who all played for Leamington FC. A lot of the players also played together for Westlea Wanderers. Goal-scorer Leaver was presented with the man-of-the-match award by Coventry City defender Jordan Clarke.

Whitnash Neil Stacey, Jack Taylor, Craig Watkin, Lee Scott, John Blunsom, Henry Leaver, Luke. Cole (Paul Wilkinson), Mike Ellis (Howard Forinton) Josh Cole, Ross Briscoe (Glenn Webb), Ryan Billington Subs: James Urquhart, Andy McKinley.

Whitnash Town now compete in The Coventry Alliance Football League, which is a Saturday league. Whitnash United (Sunday team) play in the Tracey Thomas Leamington and District Sunday League.

Cubbington Albion

West Bromwich Albion legend Tony (Bomber) Browns first game for the Baggies was against Cubbington Albion, he was playing for the Baggies fourth team he was about fifteen. This match would have been about 1961; Tony recalls that he got kicked a bit! Tom Lewin an Albion fan told me he saw him play a few times he is his all-time favourite player.

Carl Goddard

Carl was an outside right for Cubbington Albion and he played in that match against West Bromwich Albion, I asked him a few questions about his football career.

What are your memories of playing for Cubbington Albion?

I was in that Cubbington side in 1961 that played West Bromwich Albion. The Warwickshire Combination had four League teams in and when you played against them there would be a mixture of current internationals and players that were being watched to see if they were in the reckoning for introducing into the first teams.

What famous players have you played against?

Schofield, Brown (Birmingham City). Hope, Millard (West Bromwich Albion). Atkinson (Aston Villa).

How long did you play for Cubbington?

I played for Cubbington Albion for about six years

What other teams did you play for?

Lockheed Leamington's youth and A team's for four years and Radford (Coventry) one year. Lockheed works team one year

Did you play against Ron Atkinson what was he like?

Ron Atkinson was a wing half, quite a good player and very vocal.

Johnny Schofield who Carl played against was a goalkeeper from Atherstone; he played local football before signing for Birmingham City in 1950. Johnny was mainly a backup for legendary Blues keeper Gil Merrick throughout the decade becoming first choice in 1959. In 1960 and 1961 Birmingham City got to the final of The Inter-Cities Fairs Cup and Johnny played in the finals against Barcelona and Roma.

Bobby Hope a Scottish international midfielder / inside forward was one of West Bromwich Albion's star players of the 1960s.

Ron Atkinson doesn't need much introducing, more famous as a manager but he was a good player too. Nicknamed "The Tank" he was an inspirational captain for Oxford United in the 1960s.

Thank you for your time Carl

Micky Fox

I contacted Micky's son Steve by email and asked him about his dad's career.

Micky moved to Cubbington from Bolton approximately in 1951 aged about six years old. He started playing for Cubbington Albion aged fifteen which was about 1960. The team was Semi-professional at the time, and they played in Cubbington Village on the Broadway, near the Village Hall. Micky always played left wing, as he was naturally left footed.   He was accepted at a selection process along with Royce Davies and although they were both fifteen. A lot of the other players were in their twenties.

Micky began working at Lockheed at fifteen, where his father John Fox also worked. He Stayed with Cubbington Albion for about two seasons until he was seventeen 1963. Later in the same year he joined Standard Athletic (based in Coventry) which was a Saturday League team. Micky was asked to join following a trial arranged through their current manager at the time. Contact with this manager was made through his father, his father and the manager worked together at Lockheed. It was a bit of a trek each Saturday from Leamington Bus Station to Pool Meadow, Coventry. No coaches then!!

Standard Athletic played in the Coventry and North Warwickshire League. Micky recalls one player around this time called Barry Chadband who played in midfield he rated him.

Micky recalls Standard Athletic reached a Cup Final versus South Leamington in the mid-1960s. There was a dressing room rumour that Micky was on his way to South Leamington immediately after this game, and as such when he arrived at the ground he found he was out of the team, ignored by the players, and not even substitute – so he went home. They won and he was later advised he had a Championship winner's medal awaiting him. He refused it, and so I understand his Dad had a few stern words for the manager – whom he still worked with!

Micky played for Lockheed Leamington, Kenilworth Rangers, Stratford Town and Saltisford Rovers in the 1960s. He moved to South Leamington late 60's and pretty much stayed there until he finished 1972. Torn knee ligaments – long before the days of key-hole surgery!

Through this time he played many times against South Leamington and got to know their players – either facing against them, or playing alongside them with a different team. Around the time, players often played for a few teams at the same time. There didn't seem to be a restriction of one club i.e. played for a different club Tuesday night, Thursday night and then on Saturday, so he therefore played games for different teams, without being firmly associated to one team

The manager of South Leamington was Brian Knibb, during the late 60's. He knew this man very well and said that he was known, and reputed through the local area, through his managing and football contacts

Micky spoke very highly of Tony Partridge (goalkeeper) who he thinks they recruited from Flavels when Tony worked there. They played together for many years at South Leamington. Terry Keen was a great player as was Ray Hopkins. He really rated Tony and said he thinks he may have had a trial for Coventry City and may have signed semi-professional forms for them at the time. They both ended up working at Lockheed together, both were firm friends, and still are to this day. Micky recalls having a trial himself for Walsall for about eight weeks in the early 1960s.

Lockheed's team was full of ex-professional League players who now worked for the company including Brian and Roy Bradley.

Memorable matches

5th March 1966

Standard Athletic score eight!

Standard hammered Coventry Hood and Sidescreen 8.1. Simpson, Fox, Plummer and Ireland with the goals.

2nd December 1967

Kenilworth Rangers win entertaining match

Micky Fox helped Rangers beat GEC 4.3, he scored the third goal. At half time the score was 2.2, Kenilworth's goalkeeper was Bob Steane who would play for Lockheed Leamington.

Thank you Mick and Steve for your help

Cubbington news stories

People from Cubbington, Warwickshire are known as "Ear Biters" and here is why, a report from the Warwick and Warwickshire Advertiser

9th October 1920

John Edward Cyphus a farm labourer from Cubbington summoned William Samuel Skelsey a Sawyer also of Cubbington for assault on 2nd October in Cubbington.

There was a cross summons, Skelsey appeared in the court heavily bandaged around his ear and head he alleged that Cyphus had bitten his ear partially off during a fight after a football match. It was a match between

Cubbington and St Marks both men pleaded not guilty. Cyphus was a spectator and had words with a player called Cleaver who was sent off then Skelsey started the altercation, Cyphus claimed that it could have been glass which caused Skelseys ear damage. Skelsey alleged he was bitten by Cyphus.

The final outcome decided by the Chairman of the Bench who were off the opinion that Skelsey started the fight and was fined 10s. The case against Cyphus was dismissed.

25th April 1953

Cubbington win Telegraph Junior Cup

Cubbington beat Daimler Reserves 1.0, Woodward with the winning goal set up by Waterhouse.

Cubbington Albion – J Cleaver, Heath, Hall, C Cleaver, Hughes, Barrett, Bugg, Kerry, Woodward, Waterhouse, Talbot

24th February 1962

Cubbington Albion score seven goals in second half

Warwick Town were beaten seven nil by Cubbington Albion with goals from Norman Hartley who scored four, David Farmer two and Ivor Hunt one. Norman came from Lockheed to Cubbington, Carl Goddard recalls he played inside right to me, his brother Harold played centre forward. Norman was a great player he guided me along my earlier career.

11th September 1965

Cubbington go nap

Cubbington beat Kenilworth 5.0 with goals from Payne two and one each for Goddard, Ashmore and Royce-Davis.

11th May 1979

Cubbington Albion Juniors make history

The village youngsters who are members of the Under 16 section beat senior team Ryton Albion Reserves 5.1 to reach the V L Edmonds Cup Final. Cubbington's goals were scored by Marcus Easterlow, Tony Marsh, Tony Lambert, Maurice Sleem and Shandy Kang.

Cubbington Albion also included central defender Billy Jawandha in their team. Billy played for Leamington in the 1987/88 season he has been manager of Hellenic League Division Two South team Taplow United for over twenty years.

Lillington

Ryan Cranton

Lillington Juniors FC adult team compete in the Tracey Thomas Leamington & District Sunday Football League. However this is only one aspect of the club, I contacted Founder, Director, Head Coach, Child Welfare Officer Ryan Cranton to ask him a few questions about his career in local football.

Can you tell me about your junior career what teams you played for?

I started playing football when I was seven for my school team in a small village; we were a very small school with only a handful of boys who were interested in football. I didn't start playing for a team outside of school until U10s when I started with St Peter's Celtic. I stayed with St Peter's Celtic until U14s, having started as centre half at U10s and then moving to striker and scoring 89 goals in one season. I then spent two years playing for Stratford Town at U15s level; I also played for Stratford Town Reserves too

What senior teams did you play for and your preferred playing position?

When I was fifteen I joined VS Rugby (now Rugby Town) and played for their U18 midweek floodlit team. I stayed with the Youth team at VS Rugby for four seasons, when I made the transition to the VS Rugby Reserve team and then to the first team. Towards the end of my time at VS Rugby, I was loaned out to Stratford Town first team. When I was in the U16s team, I sustained my first knee injury and tore cartilage in my right knee, when I returned to playing I started playing in central midfield to regain fitness and it was that position I spent the rest of my career playing.

It was during my youth time at VS Rugby where I also had experience of playing at three professional clubs - Coventry City, Newcastle United and Barnsley. I was offered an YTS place at Barnsley, however having spent time in Barnsley I was very reluctant to move there and turned down the offer. The following season Barnsley were promoted to the Premier League, the first time they had been in the top division for 100 years. When I was sixteen I moved from Stratford Town to Alveston U16s and played for Alveston Reserves too. When I was eighteen I started playing Sunday morning for Westlea Wanderers. I spent a few seasons at Westlea, before moving on to play for Leamington Hibs in my early 20s.

Upon leaving VS Rugby, I played on a Saturday for a number of clubs including Kenilworth Town, Coventry Sphinx, Leamington Hibs and Southam United. When I was twenty four I sustained a serious ACL tear in my left knee, as well as cartilage damage and the ligament in my knee was reconstructed and I was told to stop playing football. I continued to play football on a Saturday and then on a Sunday morning with friends. In my late 20s, before my ACL reconstruction gave way during a game which has left me with no ligament in my left knee and the prospect of needing knee replacement when I was older. I played again on a Sunday morning when I was about 35 for a few years but stopped playing competitively every week when I was 39. I now play indoor football every week for fun and a coaches v parents game each year in the summer as I don't think I could every bring myself to retire completely! Despite my early years playing as a striker, my preferred position was central midfield.

How did you get into management and coaching I believe that you were at Racing Club Warwick and Kenilworth Town?

I got in to management/coaching at Racing Club Warwick through a friend of mine, who was brought in at the time to run the Reserves. At the start of him time at the club, he was away for a long period pre-season and as his assistant I took over the Reserves in his absence.

While he was away the first team manager was let go and his replacement asked me if I wanted to move over to the first team and be his assistant. This was an opportunity I couldn't turn down. In short space of time, the first team manager was also let go and I found myself going from being an assistant in the reserves to being asked to take over the first team in October 2009. I appointed Scott Easterlow as my assistant at the time and it's great to see him doing so well as the current first team manager. It was an incredibly hard challenge, as we were the only team in the league without a playing budget and there was a lack of support at the time from those involved at the football club. The club were on the verge several times during my twelve months of folding completely! However my Dad and I spent many hours ensuring that the club was sustainable and were able to carry on, something we were very proud of doing in extremely difficult circumstances.

After Leaving Racing Club Warwick in October 2010, I was asked to help out at Kenilworth Town with Kev Kingham. Kev is someone that I have always had a lot of respect for. I spent some time as coach at the club before a change in personal circumstances meant that I could no longer commit to the role as I would have liked to.

Could you tell me a bit about how you started Lillington Juniors and how it has grown and your role now?

As a father of a young family I wanted somewhere for my youngest son to play. This was in 2013 when he was seven. I couldn't find anywhere and so I decided to start up my own junior football club. We had six teams in the first season, including an U8s team for my son. They are a team I have coached and still do to this day and they are now U13s level and playing 11-a-side for the first time this season.

To be honest, I never expected the club to grow to the numbers we have today or thought of it as anything other than something I would do at the weekends. After just one year, I found that the football club was impacting my work career and realised that either the football club would have to stop or I would need to leave my job. I decided, due to popularity of the football club, to leave my job and start up my own coaching company called Top Corner Coaching so that my bills could still be paid and I could still devote time to the football club.

We had only six children attend our first coaching session in October 2013. Now in our sixth season, we have thirty teams and almost 400 young players and thirty five coaches representing the football club every week. It has been an incredible growth, both in terms of numbers and reputation, and this has been down to our fantastic group of coaches. Our club's ethos of not holding trials and not just picking the "good players", but instead allowing all children the opportunity to play football.

Over the past three years we have developed our girls section too and we now have seven girl's teams. I started the football club along with my wife Jodi and my father Bob. We are a football family who has spent hours and hours creating football opportunities for young players. We turned our house in to an office and storage facility for equipment; we are so pleased to see so many children now taking up the opportunity at the football club. My role now involves the day-to-day running of the football club as well as coaching an U13 team and new U8 girls' team and being Head Coach and helping other coaches.

How long has Top corner coaching been going? Could you also give me an overview of what you do?

Top Corner Coaching started by offering football only, however over the years we now offer a variety of sports to schools in the area. Also delivering PE lessons, PPA cover and after school clubs. We also run school holiday clubs; host sports' birthday parties and I personally deliver one-to-one football coaching as an FA Level 3 coach. I will soon complete my UEFA B course too.

Did you play with any well-known players at Newcastle United or Coventry City?

I played with Dave Bennett the ex-Coventry striker, when I was at Stratford Town. When I was at Coventry it was mainly in the youth team. I did play with John Curtis when I played for Warwickshire; he went on to play for Manchester United, Barnsley, Blackburn Rovers and Leicester City amongst other clubs as well as being capped at U20 level for England. I also played with Marc Bridge-Wilkinson in the same Warwickshire team who went on to play for Derby County, Port Vale, Bradford City and Carlisle United. I got through several stages to reach the final trials for England schoolboys when I was fifteen.

When I was at Newcastle it was a surreal experience and one of the best moments in my life, as I'm a life-long Newcastle fan. I was there during the Keegan-era and Keegan coached us on a number of occasions.

Due to the club's achievements at the time when we were fighting for league titles and cups. We used to get approximately 4,000 watching the training sessions on a Friday and I actually signed autographs for fans during my time there.

It was brilliant and quite overwhelming at the same time. I played with the likes of Peter Beardsley and Les Ferdinand during training. I actually remember spending some time in the physio room, after twisting my ankle next to Les Ferdinand and Malcolm Allen.

Thank you very much Ryan and all the best for your continued great work.

Bishop's Tachbrook

Mick Murphy

I asked Mick a few questions on Facebook about his time with Bishop's Tachbrook.

How long did you play for them?

I was involved with Bishop's Tachbrook for almost thirty five years (My first game was in 1968) as a Player, Captain, Treasurer and Secretary over the years.

Did you play in a cup final for them at the Windmill Ground?

Yes I played in one of the last games to be played at The Windmill Ground. Cup Final V The Green Man. Bishop's won 4.2 if My memory serves Me correctly. I scored the third goal. Unfortunately I can't recall which Cup it was

Who would you say were the best players when you were at the club? I believe Ian Walker and John Glenn were both managers?

Indeed they were Ed. Three decades is a long time to remember, but here goes!

1970's, - Dabber Broughton, Paddy Crowley, Kelvin Evans.
1980's - Ajit Braich, Trevor Bradley, Pete Harrison, Alan Staniforth and Pete Murphy.
1990's Ian Walker took over as Manager and bought a wealth of youth to the club. Excellent players were Paul Lea, Simon Walker, Paul Coleman and Pete Harrison.

Pete Harrison was an outstanding goal scorer for over fifteen seasons with The Brook, as was Paddy Crowley who spent almost twenty years with us.

There are three other 70/80's stalwart's that spring to Mind are midfielder Dave Muddeman. Defenders -Tony Hodgekins & Kevin Else. They were all Tachbrook Boys and also served The Club in various capacities. Chris

Read, John Leach (RIP) and Tony Winters are three of the original lads that started up the team back in the 1960's.

Thanks for your time Mick

Current team

A fantastic first season for Bishop's Tachbrook FC they won Division Three and reached the Cancer Research UK Charity Invitation Cup final on Sunday May 19th 2019 but lost 5.3 to Westlea Wanderers. Adam Knight scored a hat rick; the striker had an amazing season scoring thirty goals.

Chris Pheasey

I contacted Bishop's Tachbrook's secretary on Facebook and asked him a few questions about the team.

This was the team's first season?

Yes it was the club first season and me and a couple of mates Roberto Ciurlia and Daniel Bates decided to set up a team Daniel has many years' experience in the game as a player and manager. So he was a massive part of the team and he knew players so the three of us started rounding up lads who we knew and we had a fantastic pre-season and an even better season.

You all must be so delighted to win the league, what do you put the success down to?

I couldn't have been any prouder of my players and everyone who put in the hard work for the team. I put the success down to everyone in the team sticking together and playing as a team even when we was behind. And the captain Dan Bates making sure everyone was doing their job on the pitch.

I know that the result didn't go your way but must have been great playing against Westlea in the cup final, Adam with a hat rick, must be well proud?

Playing against Westlea Wanderers and only narrowly missing out on winning the cup proved we are a team that will play team at the highest standard in Sunday league football and compete and I think Westlea was surprised how well we played against them most team 5 - 1 down would give up but we didn't we battled to the end. Adam Knight was a different class all season and proved how good of a player he is. The best striker in the Sunday league without a doubt. Also our sponsor Anthony Birmingham has been a massive part of the team as he has funded the team with kits balls training gear so we really couldn't have done it without him either.

Thanks for your help Chris and I hope that you achieve promotion this season.

Hampton Magna FC

Jack Mancini

I contacted Jack on Facebook and asked him a few questions about his time as manager and the team's success last season.

I believe that Hampton Magna FC is now 50?

Yes it's our 50th year this year. We won the Division Three Cup last year and have been promoted to Division Two.

Could you tell me the goal scorers and the XI that played in the Cup final?

Luke Malin Mike Jefferson (1) Charlie Woodward (c) (1) Nick Welch, Paul Rose, Jason Holland, Jamie Barnes, Sunil and Ash Turnbull Adam Timlin (3) Trav Lea

Subs - Alex foster Sam Perry (1) Tommy Wyatt

Sam Perry is the son of well-known Leamington footballer Neale Perry.

Who did you manage before Hampton Magna?

The last team I managed before Hampton Magna was Warwick Wanderer's Reserves in 2015/2016 and we achieved the division five double and didn't lose a single league game.

Thanks for your time Jack

Chapter Six – Works teams

A look at some of the great works teams in Leamington and Warwick.

Flavels

Gordon Simms

A Leamington kid, Gordon was a right winger he is part of a small club of players from the town to play in the football league.

Gordon was with Flavels Athletic from 1953 until 1955 he previously played for St. John's Leamington and South Leamington FC. In 1955 Gordon signed for Coventry City he made one first team appearance in October 1957. Gordon had a spell at Notts County but didn't play for the first team; he later played for Nuneaton Borough, Lockheed Leamington and Warwick Town.

I am friends with Gordon he is gentleman, I asked him about his time with Flavels he has fond memories of playing with Ted Roberts. It was Ted who recommended him to Coventry City. Gordon is a member of the Coventry City Former Players association and often attends matches with Ken Brown, Ian Goodwin and Graham Walker. Ken remembers playing against Flavels in the mid-1950s he played for Coventry City's reserves A and B teams he told me Ted was a great in the air and heading the ball.

Ted Roberts

Ted was a great inside forward he is Coventry City's third highest goal scorer of all time with eighty six goals, he signed for The Bantams in 1937. In 1939 Ted was twenty three so he lost his best years as a player during the war years but he remained at Coventry until 1952. Ted was great in the air; he is certainly one of the clubs all-time greats.

Ted in the news

31st August 1955

Lockheed Reserves win thrilling derby match

Lockheed Reserves beat Flavels 5.3 in a Warwickshire Combination match. Hartley scored three for the Brakes, Grimwood and Lovering (own goal). Ted Roberts, Gordon Simms and a Mick Lane (own goal) for Flavels.

3rd December 1955

Flavels win at Coventry Amateurs

One nil down at half time, Flavels hit back to win in the second half thanks to goals from Roberts and Henn

Dudley Roberts

I contacted Dudley (Teds) son via email, Dudley was a good striker in his playing days

Do you remember seeing your dad playing?

I never saw Dad play for Coventry City I was as about six or seven when he finished in 1952. Dad went on to play for Kings Lynn, he didn't stay very long the traveling was too much and they released him. I think he went to Banbury Spencer next he used to take me to all home games Les Latham played there too, next was Bedworth Town do not remember years. I didn't know he played for Flavels and did you say he worked there. I also remember seeing him in Charity games against young Sean Connery and Tommy Steel. I think he went back to Coventry City in 1958-60 near that and Finished when Jimmy took over 1961. He died in 1970 in Coventry aged fifty three.

What are your memories of your time with Coventry City, I read about a match when you scored twice v Charlton Athletic in 1965.

I signed Professional in 1963 by Jimmy Hill and got into first team in 1965. I made my debut away at Preston a week later making my home Debut against Charlton Athletic. This was on my twentieth birthday we won 3-1, I scored two first half goals. 1 still can't remember scoring my first goal as it after clashing heads with George Curtis. I remember the second one and I have got a picture,

At one time had got six in eight games then got injured. It was hard to get back in team Jimmy had left and Noel Cantwell sold me to Mansfield in March 1968. It worked out great. Mansfield I had seven great years 200 games 80-90 goals. We enjoyed some wonderful FA Cup games Leeds away Liverpool home and away, they had all the top players playing.

Would you say that your most famous match was the FA Cup game for Mansfield against West Ham in 1969? A famous win for the Stags. Teammate Jimmy Goodfellow later played for AP Leamington.

My best game has to be beating West Ham in 1969 with Bobby Moore and the World Cup winners playing beating them 3-1 great night as you said with the late Jimmy Goodfellow playing for us We got beaten in Quarter final by Leicester City 1-0

26th February 1969

Mansfield Town 3.0 West Ham United – FA Cup Fifth Round

Third Division Mansfield Town produced a shock by knocking out First Division West Ham United who fielded a strong team full of England internationals. Roberts, Keeley and Sharkey scored the goals in this famous win. West Ham United winger Harry Redknapp would later become an AP Leamington player.

Mansfield Town: Dave Hollins, Sandy Pate, Mick Hopkinson, Johnny Quigley, Stuart Boam, Phil Waller, Ray Keeley, Nick Sharkey, Bob Ledger, Dudley Roberts, Jimmy Goodfellow

West Ham United: Bobby Ferguson, Billy Bonds, Bobby Howe, Martin Peters, Alan Stephenson, Bobby Moore, Harry Redknapp, Jimmy Lindsay {Ronnie Boyce}, Trevor Brooking, Geoff Hurst, John Sissons

Fred Keeble

Fred was an inside forward who played for Coventry City, Notts County, Grimsby Town and Albion Rovers playing with football legends Jock Stein and Tommy Lawton. Fred played non-league football for Bedworth United, Nuneaton Borough and Lockheed Leamington. In 1953 he was player-manager of Flavels, on 26th September 1953 they won their first game of the season a 4.3 win at Warwick Town. The match report said that Keeble didn't put a foot wrong, Flavels goals were scored by Randell, McKinley, Fletcher and Spacey. Flavels didn't have a great end to 1953 and found themselves second from bottom of the league.

Paul Wildman

I asked Jodie Wildman a couple of questions about her dad's career, Jodie's uncle Bob Damp also played for Flavels.

Could you tell me a little bit about your dads career, what teams he played for and where his nick name peanut came from?

My Dad (Peanut) Paul Wildman started playing at school in the 1970's for Myton High he also played for Avon Rovers, St. Peter Celtic, Flavels, Bulldog sports, Bishop's Itchington, AP works,

Westlea Wanderers (don't think there was a team he didn't play for!) They won leagues one, two, three and four; he was quite well known in Leamington as a very good keeper.

Some say he should have gone professional! His nickname peanut came from his friend when he was having his hair cut (he had quite a lot of hair) one time he was having it cut and his friend was with him, the barber took the sides short and his mate shouted to him he looked like a peanut so it stuck from there.

Was your dad always a goalkeeper?

Dad was always a goalkeeper (says this is because he couldn't run fast!)

hank you Jodie, there is more about Jodie's football career later in the book.

Winsams

Winsams were the dominant team in local football. In the 1968/69 and 1969/70 Leamington Sunday League seasons Winsams beat Westlea Wanderers to the championship. Winsams had possibly the most potent strike force in Sunday football with Barry Whitlock and Dennis Farr.

Eric Canning

A full back in his playing days I asked Eric a few questions about his playing career.

Hi Eric could you tell me what Junior and Senior teams you played for?

I played for St. George's boys club then North Leamington juniors after this I played for Whitnash followed by Southam United then on to Winsams

When did you play for Winsams?

I played for Winsams on Saturday for two years in the Coventry Alliance Premier we shared Racing Clubs pitch this was 1969ish

Winsams were a great side in the late 60s what players stood out for you during your time there?

George Ellard, Keith Orme

George Ellard's brother Victor also played for Winsams, George played briefly for Lockheed in 1967.

Thanks for your time Eric.

Pottertons

Pottertons FC have had some fine players and teams over the years; I come across a team photo what Tom Lewin posted on a Facebook group of Pottertons FC 1969. This team included many good players including Paul Garner, Bob Phillips, Terry Thwaites, Dennis Woodhead and George Burrows. England cricketer Eddie Hemmings also played for them in the late 1960s / early 1970s.

Pottertons in the news

27th August 1966

George Burrows to lead Pottertons attack

Former Lockheed Leamington outside left of the late 1950s George Burrows is Pottertons main player for the new Works League. Ernie Conway is manager, centre forward Graham Meakin is expected to score a few goals.

29th October 1977

Pottertons top of the league

Pottertons enjoyed a fine start to the season, top of the Alliance Premier and unbeaten; they recently beat leaders Massey Ferguson 4.3. Manager Pete Deakin has assembled a strong squad including fine goalkeeper Terry Thwaites, Barry Proctor and John Glenn. Duncan Gardner scored the winning goal in the match against Massey Ferguson coming back from three goals to win.

14th April 1979

Pottertons cause cup upset

Pottertons beat Willenhall Social in the Coventry Evening Telegraph Cup 2.1, Willenhall were unbeaten since October 1977. Mick Rainbow and Arthur Lucey scored for Pottertons.

Ajit Braich

I spoke to Ajit on the phone and he told me a bit about his football career. Ajit was born in India, at a young age he moved to Warwick and he then played for West end Youth Club aged fifteen. By the mid-1970s Ajit moved to Sydenham and was a youth player for Racing Club Warwick. In his early playing days he was mainly a left back then he became a sweeper later on.

Ajit played Sunday League football for Khalsa for about two or three years, a season for Whittle Wanderers and nine or ten years with Westlea Wanderers. Ajit also played Saturday football for Pottertons, Stratford Town and Racing Club Warwick.

Ajit talked about some of the great players he played with these included Cliff Morby, Ian Montgomery, Bill Draper, Micky Clarke and Don Grantham. Ajit also played in a pick of the league XI in the late 1970s.

During his time with Westlea, Ajit played with Ian Walker and towards the end of his career Ian's sons Ashley and Simon.

In January 1978 Ajit was part of the Potterton International team who were top of the Coventry Alliance Premier Division. Under manager Pete Deakin they had a very good team – Terry Thwaites, Roger Talbot, Alan Stacey, Ajit Braich, Barry Proctor, Paddy Hill, Paul Garner, Paul Coleman, Duncan Gardner, Barry Whitlock sub Chris McCarthy. Pottertons finished third in the end but it was a great achievement to do so, all of the players were well known in local football.

Ajit began his coaching career with Stratford Town's second team and he gained his FA qualifications at Lilleshall. In the mid-1990s he worked as a community coach at Coventry City when Phil Neal was manager. Outside football Ajit worked for the East Midlands Electricity Board for over twenty years and is a very keen golfer.

Ajit now lives in Canada and has had different roles in football including a spell at Vancouver Whitecaps, Ajit Braich Soccer Academy, and a consultant with South Burnaby and technical director with South Delta.

Ajit's brother Bindy also lives in Canada; Bindy was also a good player especially for Avon Rovers.

Avana Sports

Mick Mackey

Avana sports we're a Sunday team previously known as Fleur de Lys (the pie factory Emscote road) In the 1970s they had a good team. Notable players from that era were Mick Mackey, Robin Hood, Ken Lambert and Paul Cooke. In another chapter Steve Mancini talked about a teammate Mick Mackey. I contacted Mick via Twitter and email and asked him a few questions; he is former Leamington and Racing Club Warwick striker Ben Mackey's dad. Mick played junior football for St Peters Celtic who had a few good players in the early 1970s like Paul Smyth and Gerry Gleeson; they once won the Lockheed Cup beating Ajax.

Do you have a favourite of Ben's matches?

Just trying to pick my favourite game of Bens is too hard there's too many but my favourite season is at Hemel Hempstead where he broke their goal scoring record and won the SLP.

Did you have any trials with any football league teams?

I never had any trials but I remember back in the day the Avana sports manager Bill Dell turning up at my door telling me AP Leamington wanted to sign I was so excited it was when Jimmy Knox was manager and they were a top non-league, what a let-down when I turned up to train and realised it was in fact AP works Saturday team.

Do you have a favourite match and goal for Avana?

Favourite game/goal for Avana is difficult so many forgot most but one that I always remember is a game against Red Lion Kineton, after scoring 6 one of their players while running past me off the ball gave me a crafty punch, I turned and returned the favour. The ref had seen nothing but our linesman Dennis Fleming was flagging furiously to get his attention and after he told him what happened we were both sent off, when I asked Dennis why he did that he said "sorry mick he is my bother in law "happy days.

What were Paul Cooke and Robin Hood like as players?

Me and Cookie worked together and he was my strike partner great player, Robin and his older brother Dave were good players Dave was hard tackling no nonsense player I think from midfield Robin was a different player fast and tricky think he played wide, happy days

Mick played for Avana Sports when he was sixteen until he was thirty, then finished off playing for Warwick Railway Pub.

Avana Sports in the news

22nd February 1975

Avana Sports win thrilling cup final

Flavels 4.5 Avana Sports (after extra time) Division Four Cup Final

Paul Cooke got the winner in extra time for Avana Sports, they had led 4.2. Steve Hawkes scored three for Flavels, Ian Treadwell also scored. For Avana Sports Cliff Mancini and Paul Cooke both scored two goals, Mick Mackey the other goal.

24th April 1976

Avana Sports beat leaders

Avana beat Flavels 3.0 thanks to a Mick Mackey brace and one from Robin Hood.

Ford Sports

A strong Leamington Sunday Premier League side in the mid-1970 .Notable players include Norman Brison (Lockheed Leamington) Duncan Gardner, Mick Clarke, Mick Murphy and Tommy Aitken.

Tony Sollis also played for Ford Sports he became sports editor of the Leamington Observer. His dad Tom helped run this team and played for fords in the 50s.

I contacted another good Fords player of this era David Vicary on Facebook to ask him a few questions.

David Vicary

Hi David did you play with Duncan Gardner At Fords Sports?

I played with Dunc at Fords and also at Pottertons for a number of years before he went on to bigger and better things. Remember that, he was blessed with great pace, was physically strong and could finish well. Defenders (at all levels) found him a real handful.

What other teams did you play for?

I started playing for Kenilworth Rangers aged around seventeen when my Dad managed the White Lion in the town. I followed that by playing for Massey Ferguson in the Coventry Works League. This was at the time of permit players who had League experience and who were basically given jobs by large companies and paid "expenses" to play football for their teams. At Masseys we had a centre half from Northampton Town, a midfielder from Coventry City and a goalkeeper who had a number of years' experience of Scottish League football. Funnily enough the Coventry lad also nearly signed for Torquay (like Duncan) when Frank O'Farrell managed them, unfortunately his attitude wasn't right so they decided not to take him. I played for Pottertons for many years, after I started working for the firm, with a large number of local 'stars' like Cliff Morby, Micky Clarke, Duncan, Steve Montgomery, Ian Montgomery and Pete Deakin amongst others. I Sunday football was always interesting because the Potts lads played for a few of the top Leamington sides so faced each other regularly on wet and cold Sunday mornings. My teams were Ford Sports, St Dominic's and Leamington Southend with, I think, one season at Whittle. I broke both ankles, thankfully not at the same time, playing Sunday football so gave that up first. Favourite time

Do you have a favourite match that you played in?

Favourite time was playing for Coventry Service of Youth representative team when I was around 20. We hosted St Etienne's under 21's at the Butts Stadium in Coventry one year and beat them 2-1 and then went to France to play them in a return fixture. We were supposed to play before a French League match against Rheims in front of 30,000 but our coach broke down so we arrived late. A German team from Wuppertal were touring locally so took our place for that match. Gutted about that! We did play St Etienne two days later in their stadium with about 10,000 people watching and managed to get a draw. Interestingly, three or four of the U21 side that came to Coventry the year before were playing against Rheims on that Friday night. I started playing up front but best positions were probably in the back four, mainly right back. I reckon I played every position for Potts over the year's even goalkeeper on a couple of occasions.

David talked about a John Docker; he was a youth and reserve player for Coventry City in the 1960s playing alongside Leamington lad Mick Coop and Willie Carr. A knee injury whilst on loan at Torquay United in 1967 ended his professional career. John had spells with Irish team Waterford, Rugby Town and Binley Woods.

Thanks for your help David

Leamington St John's FC (photo provided by Mark Rowlatt)

Lockheed Leamington captain before a match (many thanks Nigel Croft)

Roger Bain playing for AP Leamington in the late 1970s (Many thanks Roger Bain)

Ian Walker Westlea Wanderers legend (many thanks Chris Walker)

Westlea Wanderers winning the Cancer Cup in 1974 (Many thanks Dave Garratt)

Keith Chamley and Cliff Morby at Westlea Wanderers 50th anniversary in 2015(many thanks Wendy Morby)

Sunday Cup action between Westlea Wanderers and Bishop's Tachbrook (many thanks Rob Dent)

From left to right – My uncle Fred, me, Syd Hall and Gordon Simms.

Oken High School team circa 1961 (many thanks Chris Walker)

Leamington Hibernians under 13's team circa 1977 (Many thanks Siobhan Gordon)

Chapter Seven – Youth Football

Leamington and Warwick has a proud history of youth football. We are going to have a look at some of the great teams and players.

AP Leamington's great FA Youth Cup run

AP Leamington had a very good youth team in the 1983/84 season and embarked on a superb run in the FA Youth Cup. Manager Graham Frisby had some fine players to choose from, most would have good careers in non-league football.

Steve Hopcroft

I asked Steve a few questions about his football career; he was AP Leamington Youth team captain when we had the great cup run in 1983. A centre half Steve was playing in Northfield Town's first team at fifteen he had dual registration with AP Leamington playing in the Evening Midland Floodlit League then aged sixteen. At the time he was waiting to join the Army he was travelling from Birmingham to Leamington for matches. Steve really enjoyed his time at The Old Windmill, AP had a fine youth team under manager Graham Frisby with players like Terry Smith and Mark Rosegreen they enjoyed great wins over Northampton Town, Rotherham United and Crystal Palace. Sadly Steve missed the Southampton match because of a calf injury.

Back then AP of course had a fine first team, Steve recalls the FA Cup match with Gillingham and how close we were to causing an upset. Ironically years later Steve was working at Birmingham City when Steve Bruce was manager he was part of the Gillingham team. Steve Bruce admitted AP Leamington were unlucky to lose that match.

Steve never played for The Brakes first team, he spent time in the Army, helped run a family Fruit and Veg business in the Bull Ring then joined the Police Force. Steve also played for Worcester City, Redditch United and Halesowen Town.

Steve is now head of Academy recruitment at West Bromwich Albion; he has been at the Hawthorns for fourteen years he has previously worked for Birmingham City. Steve's work has attracted interest from Manchester United and Everton. A number of players that he discovered have gone onto become full time professionals, these include Nathan Redmond, Jerome Sinclair and Saido Berahino

The Cup run

After beating previously beating Corby Town and Northampton Town, AP Leamington's youth team faced Rotherham United whose first team play in the Third Division.

17th November 1983

Rotherham United 0.1 AP Leamington

Brakes youngsters earned a hard fought one nil win in Yorkshire thanks to a Terry Smith goal. The goal came on sixty one minutes as Nigel Shanahan crossed for Terry Smith to head home. The win was fully deserved as AP dominated for periods in the game, United did come back in search of the equaliser but AP held on for this famous win.

Brakes – Davison, Couchman, Chambers, Shearer, Chatwin, Hopcroft, Rosegreen, Shanahan, Deeley, Clutton, Smith

5th December 1983

AP Leamington 2.0 Crystal Palace

A famous night at The Old Windmill ground as Brakes youngsters knock out Second Division Eagles in the 2nd round of the FA Youth Cup. Darren Deeley scored after forty minutes and a second half penalty from Mark Rosegreen secured a great win. Palace had John Di Palma sent off, Coach Alan Smith said it was a fair result but he wasn't impressed by the refereeing. A few players in the Palace youth team squad went onto have a good career in League football. Gary Stebbing and Jimmy Carter both did not play in this match went onto have good careers especially Jimmy who played for Millwall, Liverpool and Arsenal. AP Leamington did the club and the town proud with this fantastic result.

England under 21 manager Dave Sexton was in attendance, he was impressed with AP Leamington. "They're a neat well balance side boasting a strong defence and a lot of pace up front. They'll do well"

AP Leamington - Davison, Couchman, Chambers, Shearer, Chatwin, Hopcroft, Rosegreen, Shanahan, Deeley, Clutton, Smith

Crystal Palace – Gray, W Martin, Dodman, Di Palma, Dickson, Lindsay, Haistead, P Martin, Saunders, Barry, Waters

Many thanks to Ian King the Crystal Palace historian for the match information.

7th January 1984

Southampton 5.0 AP Leamington

The score line flattered The Saints a little bit as it took them until the fifty third minute to score. Eamonn Collins was the star performer for Southampton, the Irish midfielder scored two goals and assisted for the third which was an own goal. Dixon and Burns scored the fourth and fifth goal.

Collins played for Blackpool in 1980 aged fourteen he was the youngest player ever to turn out in a professional game in England. Collins mentor was England legend Alan Ball and followed him at a few other clubs – Portsmouth, Exeter City and Colchester United. The most famous name in the Southampton team was Dennis Wise. Wisey a legend at Chelsea and Wimbledon didn't play for Southampton's first team when he was younger but returned for a brief spell in 2005-06. Defender Mark Blake played for The Saints first team and also had spells with Fulham, Shrewsbury Town and AS Cannes. John Crumplin played for Brighton and Hove Albion. When you see the calibre of players for Southampton it is fantastic that AP Leamington gave them a good game, it is a shame the final score was so harsh.

Brakes players Steve Davison and Mark Rosegreen impressed Southampton manager Lawrie McMenemy and both spent time at The Dell on trial.

Southampton – Hyde, Dixon, Burns, Blake, Collins, McCarthy, Dore (Crumplin) Wise, Richardson, Brown, Lamb

AP Leamington –Davison, Couchman, Chambers, Shearer, Chatwin, Paget (Everiss) Rosegreen, Shanahan, Deeley, Clutton, Smith

AP Leamington's youngsters did the club and town proud that season, possibly the clubs greatest youth teams. Players, staff and fans must have so many happy memories of the cup run and beating the mighty Crystal Palace on that great night at The Old Windmill.

After the cup heroics AP Leamington continued to produce good players like Dave Draper, Gary Hardwick, Harbinger Desi and Mark Davison (Steve's twin brother). These lads and some of the cup team would play for Leamington's first team and have good careers in non-league football.

Black Horse FC

Quite a few of Brakes youngsters played for Black Horse FC managed by Pete Martin who sadly passed away in 1986. I asked Pete's daughter Mandy a few questions about her dad's time involved with local football. Pete managed various teams; he started the original Leamington Ajax (not Central). They played at Pottertons as well as other teams. Black Horse had some great players who also played for Leamington, Steve and Mark Davison, Harj Dhesi, Kevin Couchman and Costa Marioudis.

Hi Mandy can I firstly ask how your dad got involved with local teams?

My dad started when I was young, I'm sure he knew a man called Cyril White back in the 60s who was getting older and he took over from him. He died in 1986 at the age of 50 whilst managing black horse. I can't remember what the first team he managed was called but can remember names like Pete Roper, Cliff Morby, Mick Clarke, and Pete Collier that was way back and remember watching them play on the pitch by Bury Road. Then remember Leamington Ajax, (not Central). His whole life was football and I can remember the winter was local, then summer was six a side competitions all over the country.

Did Black Horse and Leamington Ajax win many competitions?

His teams would go for seasons without losing a game. Big rivals were Glazepta Dynamoes and St Peter's Celtic back in the 70s. We played at Pottertons field in the 70s; I remember marking the pitch out by hand with him, ready for a match.

Some very good players played for your dad's team like the Davison twins he must have been proud of what they achieved with the Brakes?

Big names I remember Ardgi Sheri, Colin Vale, Darren and Mark Bradley, Nigel Clarke, Ian Plumbley, Dave Brockwell, my brothers Wayne and Lee Martin, Costa Maroudis Simon Cooke (great goalkeeper) . I still see men around now who want to share stories about the impact they had on their life as he gave them a purpose. Sorry to go on but he was a big name in his day along with Rolly Young, Pat Gwynne and his life was football

Mark Davison

I asked Mark about his time playing for Black Horse FC and Leamington Ajax.

Could you tell me about your memories of both teams?

Great memories from what I remember we were originally Leamington Ajax from Under 10s through to U16, we did have a fantastic team and won the Sunday league every year as a youth team.

We then as a team decided to go into adult football and were placed I think in around Division 4 which we won in the first season then next year win the 3rd and then next season the 2nd it was around then that Pete Martin died and the team quite quickly disbanded and the players went to different clubs in the area.

As you say a few have Brakes connections including Harjinder Dhesi Darren Bradley, Jaime Connell and Kevin Couchman.

Thank you for your time Mark, you and Steve were part of a golden time for youth football in Leamington.

Leamington Ajax

On the 1st of May 1972, Leamington under 12 teams Leamington Ajax and Leamington Celtic played a challenge match at Highfield Road before the First Division match between Coventry City and Arsenal. Celtic beat Ajax 3.1 and there was a photograph in the Coventry Evening Telegraph of both teams lining up and meeting Arsenal captain Frank McLintock. Ironically Frank scored the winning goals for the Gunners in a 1.0 win.

Ken Probin

Ken played in that match at Highfield Road; I asked him a few questions about his memories of that particular match and his football career.

Do you remember what it was like playing on Highfield Road?

Playing at Highfield Road was a great privilege. I had seen my first professional football match at Highfield Road just a few years before; I think it was in 1969. I went with my older brother John Shurvinton. It was

Coventry City v Wolves, a 1-0 win for Wolves with Derek Dougan getting the only goal of the game if I remember right.

I remember that when we played that day the pitch seemed so big (we were only small). Playing against Leamington Celtic would not have been my choice as they were head and shoulders the best team in our league, and probably the only team in our league that would have beaten us that day. Looking back though, it was only right that the best teams got a chance to play at Highfield Road.

Leamington Ajax played in a light blue and white strip and would have been considered to be the home team. Celtic was in their usual green and white.

If I remember right Leam Celtic went 3-0 up and we got what turned out to be a consolation goal with about 10-15 minutes to go, but couldn't manage to get a second to put any pressure on them. I came off with about 5 minutes to go to give another teammate the chance to get on the pitch. It may have been that the Coventry fans thought that I looked a bit like Willie Carr, with my ginger hair, but I got a tremendous reception as I left the pitch. I will remember that forever.

After the game the two teams lined up to clap Coventry and Arsenal onto the pitch. Frank McLintock asked me what the score was in our game as he shook my hand. I also recall not being able to get Alan Ball's autograph after the game as he was having an argument with the referee at the time great memories!

Did you play for any other junior teams and did you play senior football?

I played football for school my teams St Pauls Junior School, (1968-71) Campion School for Boys (1971-73) and Blackdown High School (1974-76). I also played a few games for the Mid Warwickshire Schools team for a season or so. During my time at school I played for Ajax for two or three seasons under Pete Martin. (1971-73 Later, I also played the odd game for

Lillington Sports. (1974) my brother Roy also played for Ajax and Lillington Sports.

After leaving school in 1976 I first played for Milton in the Leamington Sunday League (I think that what they were called) for a season. A season for Warwick West End (1977) and then a couple of seasons for Thornbank in the Leamington Sunday League (1978-79). I also played for the Leofric Hotel in the Catering League on a Sunday afternoon. (1977-79) my brother Roy also played for Warwick West End, Thornbank and the Leofric Hotel where he was a chef.

Ajax

As I remember Ajax played their games on the Recreation Ground (or the playing fields) off the Old Warwick Road, Leamington. I recall after one match I returned to get my bike only to find that it had been stolen. I remember the manager Pete Martin, a genuinely nice man, who lived in Haddon Road.

Lillington Sports

I played for Lillington Sports sometime around 1974 for a game or two. I recall I came on as a substitute in one game played somewhere to the rear of Eden Court. I remember giving away a last minute penalty for handball that resulted in a 4-3 defeat. That was a rather harsh decision as I instinctively protected my face as the ball was crossed. That could be why I didn't play more game for them!

Milton

I played for Milton for a season or two - 1976-1977 I think that the team were playing in the Fourth Division of the Leamington Sunday League. The team operated out of the Black Horse pub in Princes Street, Leamington. I recall that the team included a number of the Duncan family including, Phil and John. Also playing for a season or so was a friend of mine called Steve Dendek. A unique man called Willie Wright also played, and I think that 'Wigs' Domingo played in goal and possibly Alan Duncan, when required. The team played home games on the Recreation Ground next to the Edmondscote Sports track. I recall that the ball ended up in the River Leam on the odd occasion. We all ended up back at the Black Horse drinking beer even though I was only sixteen at the time!

Warwick West End

I played for a season for Warwick West End around 1977. My brother Roy also played for them and I recall Vernal Myton played for them. Things fell apart after we won a Division Cup semi-final 2-1 only to be disqualified from the competition for fielding an illegal player. The team played their home games off Hampton Road, Warwick.

Thornbank

I played for a couple of seasons for Thornbank - (1978-79) initially I played for the reserve team and then moved into the first team who I think we're playing in the First Division of the Leamington Sunday League. My brother Roy also played for Thornbank and I recall Geoff Grindrod, John Watson and Keith Bradley played for the first team. The team played their home games at Newbold Common. The team ended up in the Bowling Green in New Street after games where we played cards and drank beer into the afternoon.

Leofric Hotel

I played for the Leofric Hotel in the Coventry Catering League on a Sunday afternoon. (1978-79) my brother Roy was a chef at the hotel and also played for them. I recall Kim Elliott played regularly and Leamington locals Steve Dendek and Alan O'Sullivan appeared on 'special' occasions. The team played games on Abbey Fields in Kenilworth and, also played games at the Eagle Recreation Ground, Leamington.

Interesting memories not related to the Leamington Sunday League

I remember that me and my friends used to socialise in and around Lansdowne Street and Kennedy Square. (1974-76) we were usually playing football somewhere. I think it was while a few of us were carol singing locally one Christmas that we became known to John Camkin who lived in one of the big houses in the Lansdowne Circus. I think that John Camkin tried to support us in a new venture. I recall a meeting being set up in a first floor room above the Fox and Vivian, Leamington. Guest of honour was the Coventry City manager Joe Mercer. With connections to Coventry City, we were loaned some old Coventry City kit and ended up playing a game against Coventry City youth (or apprentices) at the Coventry City training ground in Ryton. We got hammered!

I also recall a small Jack Russell terrier called 'Bobby' that often joined in our games in and around Queen Street/Kennedy Square (either in the street or at one of the local green spaces). Bobby would put his head down and dribble the ball with fantastic close control and speed that most of us mere human mortals can only dream of.

In addition, I thought I would mention a few of the good Leamington area footballers that I either played with or against over the years. Johnny Woodhouse, Bobby Hancock's, Tim McKinley, Sean Commerford and Paddy Crowley. (I played with Paddy when we both represented the Brakes Machine Shop (Automotive Products) in the inter-department football competition. He is the only person that I ever played with that ran from one side of the pitch to the other just to kick a player up in the air! A very hard and uncompromising player!!

Darren Slater

Darren is currently coach of Warwickshire's under-14 Schools team. In 2018 they won the Midlands Counties League title. Players from Kenilworth, Leamington and Warwick helped the team to this fantastic achievement. I contacted Darren and asked him a few questions about his time in football.

Could you tell me about your playing career?

I started playing football at ten as a goal keeper for the 7th Cubs in Coventry at fourteen I was playing striker for the Morris works scoring a hat trick on my debut, shortly afterwards I developed Osgood-Schlitter disease in my right knee which finished my football career. In 1982 I rode for Coventry bees at Brandon stadium after winning Midland speedway junior championship in 1985 I turned professional in 1987 but due to lack of funds that was my final season.

How did you get into coaching?

I started coaching football about ten years ago with a local football club call Christ The King. I took on a team in the D league and after two seasons we were in the A league finishing runners up. I was approached by Mr R Jacques the President of Warwickshire County Football Association. I was asked if I would take on the under 14s Warwickshire County. Whilst coaching I have done my FA badges level one and two and started UEFA B. However I dropped out after spending the summer in La Manga Spain watching how the Spanish train their young players. It was completely different to what I was taught by The FA and their courses.

Tell me about the current team?

When I took this group of lads on at under 14s I was joined by Craig Collins whom I knew from Christ The King. I was also joined by Kevin Burke who came recommended from Mr Jacques. From the very beginning I emphasized that I wanted to play the Spanish way and after trails out of only forty five lads we picked twenty that we felt had both the ability and would listen to what I wanted. It's important that you know that after speaking to all the other county managers we had the lowest turnout for trails maybe because we are one of the smallest counties. West Midlands had over 200 boys apply for trials. We all knew from day one that we had something special and at the end of our first season Warwickshire County won the championship for the first time ever in its forty four year history. The following season at under15s we retained the title losing only one game all season to West Midlands. This had again never been achieved it Warwickshire County football history back to back titles and the saddest thing of all is that in Warwickshire history you are the only person who has took an interest in what we have achieved, I even contacted St George's Park to book a pitch as a surprise for the lads but after trying three or four times and having no joy I gave up. We are currently joint top in the league and in the quarter finals of the National Cup which is to be played on 11th January away to Bedfordshire. We have added to the squad this year as three of our players have obtained scholarships with Premier League clubs and Championship clubs of which we are very proud.

Thank you for your time Darren and best of luck for the rest of the season. Unfortunately the team lost against Bedfordshire however a truly great achievement reaching that far.

Glazepta Dynamoes

Glazepta were based in Ramsey Road, Sydenham. They made mainly rubber extrusions for double glazing, the company was owned by Jim Marshall. Glazepta became well known in the 1980s when they were Coventry City's shirt sponsors for the 1984/85 season. In the mid-1970s South Leamington Dynamoes became Glazepta Dynamoes, they were a successful junior football team. By the 1980s the team was known as Drill Sure Dynamoes, the team played on fields off Myton Road.

9th October 1976

Glazepta Dynamoes win nine goal thriller

Dynamoes beat Benford 5.4 with goals from Alan Bryan and Robin Harris two each, Steve Roughead also scored. Dave Yates scored two for Benford, one each for Jamie Wade and Phil Burden.

20th May 1978

Glazepta Dynamoes win Under 12 Coventry Minor League

Sponsored by Glazepta Products the team managed by Ray Russell captained by Nigel Shanahan. Nigel and teammate Ian Gorrie both went onto to play for AP Leamington FC.

Roy Russell

I asked Roy a few questions about his time in football.

Could you tell me how Glazepta Dynamoes was formed?

South Leamington FC was founded just after the war and fielded teams in the Saturday leagues of the day. Home games were played on the Eagle Rec and across the ladder bridge to the club HQ aka the Leopard.

In the early 1970s they acquired the Myton Road ground and clubhouse which had previously been used by the Leamington RFC. Lillington Dynamoes was established in 1970 to bring boys' football to the local area and helped establish the Mid Warwickshire Boys League. Around 1973 the two clubs amalgamated as South Leamington Dynamoes for both adult and junior football.

I worked with Brian Knibb who had been secretary of South Leam for many years and so took my son Andrew at the age of 9 to the club's Under 10s. The team was managed by Andy Gorrie who worked for Jim Marshall at Glazepta.

Fund raising was never easy —relying on the generosity of the families of the players Andy approached his boss Jim who kindly agreed to sponsor Sportsmanship awards for the MWBL. Next Andy and Brian managed to get Jim to sponsor the club in those days we were not allowed to have a sponsor's name on the kit. We could have the club name on display though- hence Glazepta Dynamoes.

I took over from Andy as manager in 1975 and stayed with the under 10s until they became under16s. After a couple of seasons in the MWBL we moved to the Coventry Minor League. The last match was winning the Cup final 6-1 against Coundon Cockerels at the Butts stadium.

Among my fellow managers were Brian Knibb, Jim Hemsley, Jim McGivern, Alan Watkin and the unforgettable Dave Lee. Andre Gorrie, John Hawkins, Syd Orme, Dougie Talbot (founder member), Dony Shanahan and Pete Jones were among the stalwart supporters and committee men of the club. Ted Forde became trainer/ coach as my team progressed

There were changes over the years Brian took his team to Racing Club Warwick and the senior teams ceased playing with the demise of local Saturday football.

The club became Drillsure Dynamoes in the 80s and I stayed on helping with transport etc... Until the ground was acquired by the council to enable road and canal diversion in the Myton Road area.

I had many players over the years including - Nigel Shanahan, Ian Gorrie, Daryl Hawkins, Russell Palmer, Andrew Russell , Phil Sharp ,John Baines, Euan Bennett, Darren Malin, Vince Talbot, Frank Murphy , Steven Easterlow, Graeme Bell, Rob Rennel, Steve Hussey , Kevin Jones, Richard Compton, Mark Bradley ,Phil Garner, Richard Compton, Colin Aston and for a couple of seasons Paul Doughty.

Ian and Nigel went onto greater things at senior level and Paul became a leading scorer in the US indoor league (6 or 7 a side). Rob went onto to score the winning try for Leamington in the Warwickshire Cup and Phil Sharp is well known in local golfing circles.

Players that spring to mind in the other teams include - Dave Lee Jr, Dave Watkins, Steve Bolt, Mark Curry, Mark Davison.

Amongst the refs were Vic Shepherd, Guy Reeve, Brian Aston, Dennis Compton, Kevin Cullen, and John Hawkins

Notable opponents were of course Jim Barry, George Browne, Pete Martin and Cyril Phillips

Many wonderful memories and great fun as well. We had trips to Benidorm (unofficial) and Bruges and hosted clubs from our twin towns Bruhl and Hemsteede paying return visits.

Dougie Talbot and I re-joined Brian Knibb when he took his team to Newbold Comym Arms as Redford Newbold FC in the late 1980s and this team amalgamated with Whitnash Juniors to become the highly successful RN Hodcarrier FC where we served as Chairman and Treasurer.

Thank you very much Roy for sharing your memories and your support with this book.

Brian Knibb

I spoke to Brian on the phone, as mentioned by Roy previously Brian was a manager of Glazepa Dynamoes. As a player Brian was an outside right then a full back, he played for Campion School, Mid Warwickshire schools and South Leamington the latter for twenty years.

I asked Brian which players he liked during his playing days he mentioned Johnny Butler, George Ellard, Barry Ferguson and Danny Connor. Brian recalls meeting Ian Walker who he got to play for South Leamington.

At Glazepta Dynamoes they got new kits for every team all eight of them, Glazepta owner Jim Marshall put a lot into the club.

Brian spent time helping out Bobby Hancock's at Southam. In the early days of Leamington FC reforming in 2000 he was secretary. Brian has also been a director and club ambassador he described the clubs climb as phenomenal, he goes to most home matches at The New Windmill.

Thank you for your time Brian.

Brian in the news

18th February 1961

Knibb earns draw for South Leamington

Brian Knibb gave South Leamington the lead in a 1.1 draw with Radford Social, Williams equalised for the visitors.

28th September 1974

South Leamington resign from Coventry Alliance Premier Division

Secretary Brian Knibb said that there hasn't been any interest in Saturday football, the clubs four junior teams will continue. South Leamington were formed in 1946/47 season, former players include David Woodfield, Bill Draper, George Burrows, Keith Orme, Ian Walker and Chris Elliott.

Thank you for your help Brian

St Peter's (BOSCO)

This team in the 1960s had some talented young local player like Chris Elliott, Bob Phillips, John Rose, Keith Billington, Billy Shanahan and Tom Denholme. All of these players starred in Sunday League football and went onto play for AP Leamington and Racing Club Warwick.

Avon Rovers

Avon was a successful junior team in the 1960s on the 6th December 1969 they beat a good South Leamington team 5.3 quite a few well-known local players in both teams.

Aston scored two goals for Avon Rovers, Cooke, Whittaker and an own goal. South Leamington's goals were scored by Billington, Montgomery and substitute Walker.

South Leamington – Partridge, Gill, Cramp, Shanahan, Jones, Davies, Partridge, Denholme, Billington, Montgomery, Claridge

Avon Rovers – Brinkley, Higginbotham, Horne, Elliott, Curtlin, Gould, Rose, Aston, Cooke, Adam, Whittaker

Claudio Cardellino

Claudio was part of the 1980/81 Myton School team which won the Mid Warwickshire Cup and the Warwickshire Cup. Both finals were against

Campion school. Teammates included David Moreton and Alistair Myton who both played at a good level.

I asked Claudio a few questions about his career via Facebook.

What teams did you play for?

Locally I played for Warwick Kings Head (Sunday morning In the Leamington and Warwick Sunday league) I was 14 and so was David Moreton. I played for Woodloes FC, Radford sports and social, Bishop's Itchington and Tachbrook FC, Westlea Wanderers. In 1990 when my parents owed the Malt Shovel in Bubbenhall we decided to start up a Sunday league side and I stayed with them for just over 10 years

Claudio served Bubbenhall well he scored 120 goals and played in every position including goalkeeper.

Do you play hockey too?

Yes still do, I captain Warwick Vets and their fourth team and summer league squad.

Claudio still plays a bit of football too, he played in a Leamington and Warwick Coventry City supporters club XI v Coventry City legends XI in July 2019 at the Windmill. A centenary match all proceeds to Myton Hospice.

Thanks for your help Claudio

Chapter Eight - Present Era

A focus on local football this season and recent seasons.

Leamington Ladies FC

The club competes in West Midlands Regional Women's Football League Division 1 South. In the 2013/14 season they finished a very good second in the West Midlands Regional Premier Division.

Rebecca Clarke

Rebecca is captain of the team I asked her a few questions via email about her career and time with Leamington.

What junior and senior teams have you played for?

I started my playing career at a local boys team in Coventry as there was a complete lack of female teams for my age, especially having started playing at the age of seven. I was also the only girl in my primary school team and was made captain, which went down like a lead balloon amongst the boys. From the age of nine I then started playing for Coventry City Girls. We got picked up by a volunteer on a Saturday morning on a minibus, wearing second hand kits that were too big for all of us. As soon as I was old enough I progressed to playing competitively for Coventry as a goalkeeper. After three years I left Coventry and headed to Leamington Lions where I became a striker. I finished by junior career at Solihull Borough.

I began playing senior football at sixteen for Racing Club Warwick before progressing to the higher leagues to play for the likes of Southam, Bedworth and Leafield. During this time I also captained the University of Birmingham women's team alongside studying. I have now been back at

Leamington for the last two seasons, so you could say I'm back where I started out.

What is your preferred playing position and what are your strengths?

Having played all positions throughout my junior career, my senior career has largely been as a defender. I now play centre back for Leamington and captain the side. My main strengths are my ability to read the game and being able to play out from the back. I also take lots of the free kicks and corners which helps to satisfy my urge to play up front again!

It must be awesome to captain Leamington ladies, how long have you been captain?

I was given the captaincy this season, so not long really. I have taken over from Angie Wiffen who has been a legend at Leamington over the years so it will be big boots to fill. This is something I am immensely proud of. My family have a long association with Leamington as a club with both my dad and uncle being season ticket holders, attending games for the last 50 years. Being able to lead the team out is a huge honour for all of us.

How do you think the team will do this season, has the team been together long?

This season we are hoping to perform better than last season. During the 2018-19 campaign it was all about stabilising having chosen to drop down from the Premier Division. There were lots of new players coming in and it took time for us to gel. Now that we have Paul O'Rafferty in charge as manager for the upcoming campaign, we are confident we can build on last season. We have made some really positive signings that will help drive the team forward. If we can challenge for the title then that would be great.

Jodie Wildman

Jodie is a striker for Leamington Ladies I asked her a few questions about her career

Could you tell me how you got into football and what teams you have played for?

Growing up with three brothers I grew up with football, a Manchester United fan I just loved playing. At school I was the only girl who played at lunchtime I'd be with the boys kicking a ball about! I started playing for Southam Town Girls FC in 1997, at a time when we won everything! We won the league all cups/tournaments, we were a really good side I was the highest scorer in the league. If I remember it was something like thirty six goals (average of about three a game!) I played there until I was sixteen then went back at the age of nineteen for another season.

I then found out about another local side looking for players when I was in my early 20's (Leamington Hibernian Ladies FC). I played for one season until I broke my foot in the final game of the season! I had about six years break due to injuries.

Finally at the grand old age of thirty four I thought it was time to get my boots back on! This time for Leamington Ladies FC. I chose LLFC because of the excellent facilities/staff/club a really fantastic group of ladies who all want one thing, play football and progress through the leagues. Naturally I am a striker that is my position I feel comfortable when I am upfront banging goals in! Although most of last season I was playing in a more wing/attacking role.

Have you got a favourite goal and match for Leamington Ladies?

My most memorable game of the season was the very last game at home against Kidderminster Harriers Ladies FC .I came on ten minutes before half time up front I thought great I was ready for this so hungry for my first goal of the season and it must have been my first touch I scored the goal of the season! I am now set for another season with Leamington FC hopefully bang a few more in this season!

Have you had any trials at league clubs?

No unfortunately not, maybe if I had carried on playing when I was younger who knows.

Leamington Futsal Club

Futsal is a variant of football played mainly indoors on a hard court similar to five a side. In 2018 Leamington Futsal Club was formed and are based at Newbold Comyn Sports Hall, I contacted the founder Ian to ask him some questions.

Ian Cosgrove

Could you tell me a little bit about how you started the club up and how you got into Futsal?

We got started after I was a coach at Leamington Brakes Juniors FC and the amount of games called off because of the weather was a joke. So I sat down and thought what we can do regarding kids not playing football. Everyone knows about five a side football so I picked futsal, it is hard work getting children into futsal but I will do my best.

Are you in a league? And how are the team doing?

We don't have a team at the moment we are doing training sessions to get children involved with futsal and get them active.

Do you or have you played football yourself?

My football days started at Leamington Hibs, I stayed with them for ten years great club. I had trials at Coventry City which didn't work out. I went too Portsmouth Football Club but got home sick, which was a big mistake looking back.

Thanks for your time Ian and best of luck with this venture.

Another Leamington futsal connection is former Brakes player James Husband who played for England's futsal team. Futsal is big in South America, indeed a certain Lionel Messi played for Newell's Old Boys Futsal club.

Bishop's Itchington

Ed Kostiuk

The village's Saturday and Sunday side both won their leagues, I contacted Saturday League striker Ed Kostiuk and asked him a few questions. Ed scored an impressive 51 goals during the 2018/19 season.

Did you begin your career at Leamington and how long were you there?

I started my career at Harbury Juniors. I was then scouted for Northampton Town where I spent seven years. From there I played for Leamington for two seasons in the Midland Junior Premier League under manager Curley O'Callaghan. And then went on a trial for the 1st team but injured my back in pre-season and never went back after that

What other teams have you played for?

After that I went to play for other men's teams such as Woodford United and Long Buckby.

What do you put yours and the team's success down to?

The team's success is due to a great group of lads who are all very good mates and great footballs who have gelled on and off the pitch to create a great understanding between all of us. We are all local lads who do a lot together on and off the pitch

Sunday League Champions

Bishop's Itchington's Sunday team broke Westlea Wanderers' 12-year dominance of the top flight and also won the Division One Cup, George Dutton Cup and Byfield Bethel Cup.

Bishop's Itchington's Sunday League squad

Charlie Symons ,Matty Hughes ,Tom Cooper, John Beacham Miles, Ryan, Stefan ,Joe Williams, Tom O'Callaghan ,Johnny Adair, Joel Bennett ,Michael Yeates ,Andy Yeates, Sam Wanless, Jason Bradshaw,Jonny Byrne

Tom Cooper

I contacted Tom Cooper who is the team's player / manager, Tom's dad Steve played for AP Leamington and Racing Club Warwick.

How long have you been player manager for? Been player manager since 2012/13, have been a player for either Saturday sides or Sundays or both since I was sixteen

Have you played for many teams? I also played for Stockton, Racing Club and Southam when not at university

What do you put the team's success down to? Been a good squad effort this year, we've been runners up for a few seasons but this season things were different. Coming from behind to draw 2-2 early in the season with Westlea who've won the league for twelve years gave the lads believe they could be beaten and did just that.

Tom O'Callaghan had a great season but others like Adair and Bradshaw chipped in with a few goals to a great effort all round?

I also have. Adair, Bennett and Bradshaw are three quality strikers for two positions so the competition has spurred them on! O'Callaghan was a new signing this season and made a big difference in midfield, scoring crucial goals all season.

Leamington Hibernians

An established club in local football, Hibs have Saturday, Sunday, Reserves teams that compete in different leagues. Hibs Sunday League team finished third behind champions Bishop's Itchington and Westlea Wanderers but proudly won the Birmingham FA Sunday Amateur Cup final on 14th April 2019 beating Football Futures 2013 First 4.3 on penalties after a 1.1 draw.

On the way to the final Hibs beat Penn Rovers Adults, Dudley Ajax, St Johns Rangers, Welsh Warriors and Radford Social.

The Final

Man of the match for Hibs was goalkeeper Ryan Mason making an amazing save in the penalty shoot-out. Ryan made some vital saves during the 90 minutes to keep Hibs in the game. Lloyd gave Futures the lead on 26 minutes, as the game was coming to an end Ashley Kitchen assisted Luke Swinnerton to equalise. Carl Smedley was the man who scored the winning goal in the penalty shoot out to win the cup for Hibs.

Alan Guildford

I contacted Alan and asked him a few questions about his time in football and with Hibs.

How long have you been Hibs manager and are you still playing?

I have been managing Hibs for nine seasons now commencing in 2010. I am not playing myself anymore; I played for Southam as a kid then their youth team. I then decided to go into management on a Sunday and become assistant manager at Racing Club Warwick.

Josh Blake is one of the best players I have seen at Leamington FC, It must be a boost having Josh in the squad?

It is a huge boost for the players and me to have players of the calibre of Josh Blake in the squad. Now that he is thirty eight he has adapted his game and now plays central midfield for Hibs.

Josh still gives 110% in every match and deservedly won the managers player of the year last year. He scored an important goal in our quarter final match in the Sunday Cup and scored a penalty in the cup final shootout.

Josh was approached by a number of Midland Combination Saturday managers after the final which shows they still feel he has a lot to offer.

During the early rounds when did you start to think we can win this?

I thought that it could be our year after we beat strong St John's Rangers in round four; we were literally pinned into our own half for the second forty five minutes. They missed two penalties in the game before we went through in the shootout.

Lance Clarke

I asked Lance the team's captain a few questions

How long have you played for Hibs?

This is going to be my third season with them. I've known most of the players for the majority of the time I've played Sunday League and played with a few of them for other teams.

Congratulations on winning the Sunday Amateur Cup When in the competition did you think we can win this?

To be honest I wasn't 100 percent sure until we lifted the trophy. But I would say it felt good winning the semi against a very decent team from Radford social in Coventry

What do you put the team's success down to?

I think the main reasons for success is we are a very hard working team and never really give up. We also have a lot of decent quality players and work well together.

Did you have to take a penalty in the shoot out?

I don't take pens not really a goal scorer ha-ha.

Thanks for your time Lance

Leamington Hibernians past glory

17th May 2005

Leamington Hibernian win Birmingham County FA Vase

John Paul Turpin scored a hat rick for Hibs, Steve Brandle also scored. Harj Dhesi played a starring role for Hibs.

League officials

Mark Rowlatt – Chairman

I contacted Mark via email; he is chairman of Tracey Thomas Leamington and District Sunday League.

I have heard of your grandfather but I don't know a lot about him, could you tell me about his career?

I thought I would get a start on Grandad. Edward William Rowlatt was born in Leamington on 12.12.1892.

He was always a sportsman and represented the National Schools Football team as a boy. He played for local team St Johns in the Warwick and Leamington League. He had trials with Kidderminster Harriers,

Stourbridge and Preston North End. He was selected to play for each team but the travel time was too much and it was difficult to get to fixtures, so instead at the age of 19 he signed for Leamington Town. He played 1 game and then signed up to join the Army as War was looming. He joined the Royal Engineers. He represented the Engineers at Football and helped his Regiment win the Army Cup.

He went off to War like many of his footballing mates. He was awarded the Military Medal for his action on the Somme. (49141 Spr E W Rowlatt repeatedly went out under intense shell fire and repaired breaks in the wire (telephone cables that linked the trenches). This was rare for his then Rank and he was promoted to Sergeant

He returned to Leamington and resumed his playing career. He was a reserved man and didn't discuss the war at home. His career with Leamington saw them win trophies and Titles but I do not have specifics.

He married Esther Robotham in June 1922 and had two Sons and a daughter. David was the eldest he was a fine musician. Colin a Printer by trade (My Father). And Shirley was the middle Child and she was a Tax Inspector. He died in 1952 following complications during surgery. All his Children have now passed.

Could you tell me a bit about your playing career and your journey to become chairman?

My football career started off with the twelfth Leamington (St Pauls) Cub Scouts. Mr Mann ran the team and I went up for training and on the top of Campion Hills I volunteered to go in goal. I played well and got selected and I let in six goals in that first Season.

I went to Milverton Junior School and Mr Richards selected me for the school team. I was now playing Centre Half. We won a 5-a side tournament at the Junior School on the Sydenham estate and I was delighted to receive my medal from Mick Coop who was then a Full back for Coventry City.

I then moved into the Boys League and played for Leamington Ajax under Mr Roly Young and Don Hemmingway. I represented the Mid Warwickshire boys League on a Tour to Leamington's Twin Town of Bruhl in Germany. We also played against Staffs boys I think it was, at the Old Windmill ground as an opener before a Brakes game under floodlights!

Senior School meant that I missed out on school football as Bishop Bright had no school team. It was only when we joined with Dormer that I started to play with their side. I was then asked to play with Coventry School boys and that meant training mid-week at Sidney Stringer School and Ryton at Weekends. Along with some of my new teammates I joined St Peters Celtic FC, managed by Barry Connolly. My dad had to ferry me all over the place.

I left school and moved away with work. I played briefly for a team in Coventry when I was moved there with work, but in 1985 I joined Warwickshire Police and started to play again.

The Police side was three different teams. One played in the Leamington Sunday League, the other side played in the Coventry and North Warwickshire League and the Third side played in a National Police competition. We had some considerable success and I was lucky to play at some Top grounds during my time. I have been involved with Police Football ever since and when the Alliance with West Mercia Police resulted in the loss of the pitch, the teams folded.

The Police team is now re-forming in time for the 2019-20 Season as the Alliance has collapsed and Warwickshire Police are back at Leek Wootton and we will have our pitch back.

I have been running the Police side for around twenty years now and served on the Sunday League Committee for a few years then I was asked to become Chairman about 5 years ago.

We have some great Committee people on the League and because of that we are still thriving where many other Leagues are being decimated by a lack of players coming through from junior levels to play adult football. We are looking to take the League on to the next step in the next two years now by becoming a Charter Standard League.

My personal point of view is that the game is ruining itself. Kids are spotted early and taken away to play in academies and then get dropped. They don't want to go back to face their mates saying I didn't make it and they drop out of football. We have too many other things going on that do not encourage kids to go out and play. Go down Victoria Park on a weekend and you will not see a gang of lads gathering to choose sides, jumpers for goalposts and just play football. Crime, drugs or gangs and no youth engagement. There are no simple answers but it's an epidemic that needs to be stopped before our National game goes down the swanny! Some of the bigger Metropolitan areas have lost several Leagues let alone a few Clubs.

Over the years you must have seen some great teams and players, which teams and players stand out?

I have seen some fine players in my time. Steven Waterhouse was a terrifying prospect in my junior school days. Classy players like Leo Hayes and Cassie Hancock's. Tony Lambert, Chris Brough, Mark Davison, Warren Ayers and Bob Tedds were all good quality players in the Police.

Rob Dent

Rob's role is Management Committee and Website Admin, I contacted him via email.

Can you tell me a bit about your role with the league and how long you have been doing it?

I have been a Club Secretary for a long time, and was reluctantly "coerced" onto the League Committee several years ago. This was when our division had to resort to drawing straws to nominate our division Representative for the Committee! When Mark took over as Chairman, although the league had had an online presence for a few years he was keen to make the website the focal point of the league. This would be the "go-to" place for fixtures, results, match reports, club information etc. He asked me to help get this going, and as a result I stepped up to the Management Committee and have been looking after the League's website for the last three years. Although there's still some more work to do due to the hard work of a couple of the Committee members. The clubs now trust that the fixtures, results and league tables will be accurate and up-to-date. These are published within a few hours of their matches, so the league website is now becoming the primary resource for the clubs.

Have you played football yourself? If so please tell me a little about your career?

Last season was the first one that I have not been a registered player in the league since first moving to the area twenty-five years ago! I haven't completely given up the idea of playing again, but time and injuries have taken their toll! In those twenty-five years I have been a player and player/manager in the lower divisions of the league. This is as well as a qualified referee and club Secretary for two different clubs... not to mention "retiring" many times over!

I played for IBM Warwick for ten years when I moved to this area in the early 1990s. I was going to call it a day after the IBM football team disbanded, but joined some friends at Dynamo Leamington which was a fairly newly-formed club in the bottom division at the time. Fifteen years later, (aside from a few games for Liberal Club FC), I have been with Dynamo ever since, as player, player/manager and club Secretary.

Chapter Nine - Racing Club Warwick

The club was formed in 1919 as Saltisford Rovers, honours include winning the Birmingham & District Alliance Senior Cup in the 1949–50 season. For many years until the 1960s they had a rivalry with neighbours Warwick Town.

In 1970 they became known as Racing Club Warwick, they finished sixth in the West Midland League at the end of the 1970/71 season. A fourth place finish the next season, in 1972 they Joined Midland Combination Division One, finishing a respectable seventh in the new league.

A team full of local talent they included players who played Sunday League football for Westlea Wanderers and Leamington Southend .Full back Bill Tedds had previously played for Coventry City and Lockheed Leamington. Bradley, Whitlock and Talbot all played for Lockheed Leamington or AP Leamington at some point during their career.

The 1970s

Racing Club had a fantastic squad of local players in the early 1970s.

Racing Club Warwick 1970/71 -Hyland, Tedds, Walker, Cooper, Bradley, Phillips, Rose, Farr, Elliott, Whitlock, Talbot sub Keenan

29th April 1972

Racers earn draw in top of the table clash

Racing Club Warwick earned a 2.2 draw with Armitage, Keith Orme and Dennis Farr scored for Racing Club Warwick. Roger Cope scored twice for Armitage.

4th September 1976

Boro edge Racing Club in FA Cup derby

Nuneaton Borough 2.1 Racing Club Warwick - FA Cup Preliminary round

Racing Club Warwick of the Midland Combination travelled to Warwickshire Neighbours Boro of the Southern League Premier Division. Gerry Baker's Racers side gave Boro a fright; Knight saved a last minute penalty from Morby which nearly forced a replay. Cliff Morby gave Racing Club the lead but goals from Ian Goodwin and Bob Tripe won it for Boro.

Nuneaton Borough: Knight, Stephens, Smith, Cross, Peake, Goodwin, Fleet, Lewis, Jones, Turpie, Smithers.

Racing Club Warwick: Hyland, McGoff, Maurice, Taylor, Morby, Wykes, C. Downing, Fisher, Shrimpton, Johnson, Allsop, M Taylor.

Racing Club Warwick FA Vase run 1977 / 78

Racing Club Warwick enjoyed a good run in the FA Vase in that season,

Players – Malc Hyland, Steve Cooper, George Anderson, Chris Downing, Maurice Taylor, Jimmy McGovern, Ian Montgomery, Mickey Clarke, Chris Prophet, Stuart Fisher, Alan McQueen, Roy Slade

PRE	RAUNDS TOWN	A	5-0
1	ASTWOOD BANK ROVERS	H	1-0
2	PAGET RANGERS	H	2-2
2r	PAGET RANGERS	A	1-0
3	CONGLETON TOWN	H	2-1
4	IRTHLINGBOROUGH DIAMONDS	A	0-0
4r	IRTHLINGBOROUGH DIAMONDS	H	1-2

George Anderson would become player manager for the Racers until he was sacked in December 1979, Hyland, Cooper and Slade would remain at Hampton Road until the end of the decade.

Roy Slade

I contacted Roy via Facebook and asked him a few questions about his playing career.

What junior and senior teams did you play for?

I started at Triumph Athletic straight from school. With David Heal .my dad's mate Ted Plumber took us there. ..Superb set up old Coventry works league was quality. Also played for Masseys at junior level winning several trophies... had a season at Kenilworth Town in my mid-30s winning the mid com league. Under Johnny Clarke...then I went back to Masseys then Highway club as a veteran. Winning the Birmingham junior cup...With Ian Crawley, Leon Kelly etc....

Coventry Sporting, Hinckley Town and Bedworth United at semi pro level

Bournemouth youth in FA Cup v Arsenal (Liam Brady captain)...Walsall youth and reserves...under Ronnie Allen

Who were your favourite players?

Coventry Sporting - Tony Dunk, Geoff Brassington, Johnny Davies, Derek Jones. John Sugrue (Man City later) Racing Club Warwick – Morby, Irwin, Heal, Owen, McNulty, Fisher, Duncan Gardner, Paul Coleman, Steve Cooper, Chris Prophet. At Hinckley Town Ian Crawley...

Best players played against were Liam Brady at seventeen. McGoldrick and Morley (Nuneaton Borough)

Barry Cowdrill my mate who played for Sutton Coldfield. .Barry went to West Bromwich Albion for 15 grand...

What was Dietmar Bruck like as a manager?

Brucky...loved him loved me. I recently found out that shattering my knee cost him five grand from Northampton Town. His lad told me Brucky the ladies' man...was astute tactical wise. Always up for a laugh...

What was the best team you played in?

Probably Sweeney Todd FC in the Sunday Premier, we won everything in sight for a while. On Saturdays would say RCW under Brucky.1980.until my season was cut short. By a frightening deliberate dirty tackle by a Walsall Wood left back. It took me eighteen months to kick a ball again

Triumph under George Awde in the early 1970s was superb too, winning the Premier Alliance league few times

Roy remembers the FA Vase run

A Coventry City fan, his favourite ever player is Ian Gibson. Modern era Robbie Keane

Racers stun Lockheed at The Windmill

17th April 1973

Racing Club Warwick faced Lockheed Leamington at Hampton Road in a Leamington Invitation Charity Cup Semi-Final. Ex Lockheed player and now Racing Club manager Roy Bradley named a squad of sixteen players – Hyland, Roger Talbot, Orme, Sanders, Walker, Vale, Montgomery, Hall, Bull, Ivor Talbot, Cooper, Rose, Connor, Shanahan.

Lockheed Leamington manager Jimmy Knox also named sixteen players – Steane, King, Pyle, Sherry, Cartwright, Davis, Shrimpton, Bowden, Wilkinson, Moreton, Jessop, Whitlock, Walker, Sweenie, Boot.

Over two legs the score was 1.1 therefore a replay on Saturday 28th of April which Racing Club Warwick recorded a famous 4.2 win over neighbours Lockheed Leamington. John Bull and Syd Hall put the Racers in to a two goal lead but the Brakes fought back and drew level through Steve Sherry and Tony Bowden. Bull scored again to make it 3.2 then Ivor Talbot made sure of the win, Ivor would soon Join The Brakes who would be renamed AP Leamington.

Syd Hall joined Racing Club Warwick in January 1973 after a brief spell with Banbury United. Syd played with Brian and Roy Bradley at Lockheed in the early 1960s; he would be a great signing. A midfield maestro his reading of the game and passing skills, Syd played as an outside left when he was younger but played more of a central role towards the end of his career.

Deadly Duncan goals give Racers first win of the season

23rd August 1978

Racing Club Warwick beat Knowle 2.1 thanks to two goals from Duncan Gardner, assisted by Ian Montgomery and Chris Prophet. Duncan didn't play for Racing Club Warwick for that long he signed for AP Leamington in September 1978.

The 1980s

Racing Club Warwick finished a respectable eighth in the 1980/81 Midland Combination Division One season. In the early 80s they had some good players; Dave Garratt was in goal, Cliff Morby in midfield. Up front were Alan Bryan and Steve Edgington both good strikers they formed a good partnership. Other notable players were Steve Cooper, Mark Hopkins, Gary Hannam, Paul Sinnott, Steve Hudson, Chris Chinn and Neil Thompson.

Steve Montgomery

I asked Steve about his time playing for Racing Club Warwick, the second generation of a fine local football family his dad Dave was a centre forward in the 1940s and 1950s. Steve's son Gary was a goal keeper for Coventry City in the early 2000's.

Roy Bradley was Manager at Racing Club Warwick when they were one of the top teams in the Midland Combination Premier League with his brother Brian the assistant manager. Both ex Wolves and then Brakes players.
I was a young teenager and had been spotted playing upfront in local football in Leamington by Moor Green FC (now Solihull Moors) and I signed for them when seventeen years old. It was only my second season of playing outfield as I had played in goal throughout all of my school years. When playing upfront in local football I scored plenty of goals in what at the time was a golden era for the area with lots of top quality local players most of whom were playing at Racing Club Warwick. When I signed for them; Ian Walker, John Bull, John Rose, Keith Orme, Dennis Farr, Billy Shanahan, Steve Cooper, Malcolm Hyland, Kenny Saunders, Syd Hall, Chris Elliott, Barry Whitlock to name Were all at the club.
I was an engineering apprentice at AP at the time and by chance Roy Bradley also worked there. He eventually persuaded me to join him at Racing Club Warwick. Being a local club and therefore more convenient for me than travelling to Birmingham to play for Moor Green I decided to give it a go. Looking back I have no regrets at all as I really enjoyed my time there and learned a lot from the older more experienced players who tolerated my raw enthusiasm and energy whilst always encouraging me. We had a cracking side at Racing Club Warwick made up entirely of local players and were very competitive. In my second season there I was joined by some excellent young players; Cliff Morby, Mick Clarke and Paul Coleman all spring to mind. We played AP Leamington FC annually in the Mayors of Leamington Charity Cup final. In the game I played in we drew against a Jimmy Knox managed AP Leamington team away at the Windmill ground.
This was reversed at the later end of my career when playing for Leamington FC this time against Racing Club Warwick in what turned out to be the final season at the Old Windmill ground. Again the result was a draw so honours even and therefore neither sets of fans could be too upset with me!
I had three seasons at Racing Club Warwick before being signed by

Southern League side Banbury United.

Without doubt my most memorable game for Racing Club Warwick was a home League game versus Paget Rangers which we won 5-1. I scored 4 goals and was being marked by a young central defender named Roger Brown who went on to play for Leamington before stepping up to be a successful full time pro at Fulham and several other clubs.

My goal scoring success at this level brought me to the attention of both Coventry City and Birmingham City but unfortunately I wasn't good enough to establish myself as a full time professional in England unlike my Dad Dave (Birmingham City) and youngest son Gary (Coventry City). However I did finish up playing in Australia for four years eventually being signed by one of the biggest clubs over there at the time Sydney Croatia (now Sydney FC) before returning home to England when I once again play for Leamington along with several other non-league clubs.

Thank you for your help Steve it was really nice to meet you at that Brakes match earlier in the season.

Racing Club Warwick Champions

Racing Club won the Midland Combination Premier League Champions in the 1987/88 season; it was a great season for the Racers as they reached the FA Cup third round qualifying too. They won the league by six points finishing with 56 points. John Bettles was the manager; he had also managed VS Rugby and Long Itchington. John was also a successful scout having worked for Coventry City, Leicester City, Middlesbrough and Swansea City. As a scout for Coventry City he found players David Busst, Andy Pearce and Sean Flynn from West Midlands Non-League clubs all three played for the Sky Blues in the Premiership. John's son Ian played for Racing Club Warwick in the 1987/88 season he also played for his dad at VS Rugby. John sadly passed away in April 2014 aged 77.

Racing Club had some experienced players in their squad, Malc Hyland was goalkeeper for them in 1970, and Alan Stacey previously played for AP Leamington in the late 1970s. The Racers included players from AP Leamington's fine youth team of 1983/84 Darren Deeley, Nigel Shanahan and Kevin Couchman.

Chris Coleman

I contacted Chris on Facebook and asked him about his memories of this great season for Racing Club Warwick. In the 1987/88 season he scored ten goals from forty one appearances.

What are your memories of the 1987/88 season do you have a favourite match?

Think we only lost 2 games in the League but drew a lot personally I remember 2 goals in an away win at Highgate United remember the night we got presented with the combination shield we won 2 -0 I got one of the goals against Bloxwich think we had a crowd of around 300 probably the best we had it's the only club I settled at really 2 and a half good seasons.

Did you ever play with Paul Coleman at Warwick, any relation? Paul Coleman was a valued member of the squad no relation

What other teams have you played for? I believe that you were at Swindon Town?

Other clubs Banbury United, chipping Norton, Southam United, Hinckley Athletic a knee injury finished me at 23 when possibly on the verge of going back into the pro game your right about Swindon town I was an apprentice professional from 1981- 82 I am still in touch with some of the Warwick squad we meet up once a year. Darren Deeley and my best man and still great friend.

Do you know why Racing Club didn't get promotion that season?

It was a floodlight issue we hadn't got any to get in the southern League you had to have them

A couple of famous names from Swindon's first team in 1981/82, Chris Kamara he is now known for being on Sky Sports but he was a tough tackling midfielder. Paul Rideout played for Aston Villa, Italian team Bari and scored the winning goal in the 1995 FA Cup final for Everton.

Darren Deeley

I had the pleasure of speaking to Darren, thank you Chris Coleman for helping me get in touch. Darren was top scorer for Racing Club Warwick in the 1987/88 season with twenty eight goals. A fast direct striker Darren was also part of AP Leamington's very good youth team of 1983/84 which is covered in another chapter in the book.

Darren was born in 1966 he lived in Fenny Compton in south Warwickshire, as a junior he played for Deddington Colts and a boys club in Banbury called Willy Freund. Whilst playing for the boys club he scored plenty of goals and was asked to go on trial at Wolverhampton Wanderers and Derby County. Darren was at Derby for a month which was an excellent experience for him; in 1984 Southam man Arthur Cox became manager at the Baseball Ground. Darren is the cousin of AP Leamington star Cliff Campbell and whilst at AP Leamington youth team manager Graham Frisby said to him to come and train with the first team. For a young striker it would have been very beneficial to train with Cliff and Kim Casey both of course knew one or two things about scoring goals. It took Darren the second year to get into the youth team they said the first year he was too small! In the 1983/84 season he formed a brilliant partnership with Mark Rosegreen both were key players in the FA Youth Cup run. Darren and Mark both scored in the famous win over Crystal Palace at the Old Windmill. In the mid-1980s Darren played for Bedworth United, Banbury United and also spent time at Coventry City playing for the reserve team. At Highfield Road he played with future Racing Club Warwick teammate Craig Dandridge and also Graham Rodger, Micky

Gynn and Martin Singleton, Martin is from Banbury. At Racing Club he was the first player to get a contract, being such a fast player he suffered a few hamstring injuries. Darren enjoyed his time at Hampton Road and playing with Chris Coleman, Paul(Sinno)Sinnott, Darrell White, Ian Bettles, Ian Gorrie and Craig Dandridge to name a few. John Bettles the manager was a very good motivator and later under Andy Blair who played at the very top level for Coventry City and Aston Villa. The Racers struggled in the Southern League Midland Division but stayed up for a few seasons, Darren formed a good partnership with Jamie Wootton. After leaving Racing Club he had spells at Tamworth under Sammy Chung, Stratford under Stuart Dixon and then Banbury, Brackley, Fenny Compton. Darren told me when he went to Russia for three weeks with Warwickshire schools as a fifteen year old it was certainly an experience! He has also played cricket and rugby as fly half. Whilst at Stratford Town he played briefly with Aston Villa legend Tony Morley, as a Villa fan it was very special for him. I asked Darren if he regretted not staying at Leamington a bit longer as he would have probably become a regular in the first team especially went Casey and Campbell left. Darren admitted that possibly he should have stayed a bit longer, but he may not have ended up at Racing Club Warwick and that certainly worked out well.

Thank you for sharing your memories with me Darren you should be very proud of what you achieved with AP Leamington and Racing Club Warwick.

Alan Stacey

I spoke to Alan about his time with Racing Club Warwick and his football career, a solid centre half in his playing days when he was younger he played in goal but found it boring. Alan's son Neil is still playing for Westlea Wanderers and is a coach at Racing Club Warwick. Neil also played for Leamington could play up front in defence or in goal.

Alan had two seasons with AP Leamington in the late 1970s he also played for Pottertons, VS Rugby and Southam United. A good player in Sunday football too, especially the Whittle Wanderers team of the late 1970s.

At the start of the 1987/88 season we fancied our chances under manager John Bettles he built a good side. Some of the players played together for Long Itchington on Sunday's so we had a good understanding. Alan recalls a match where the opposition attack broke down and we caught them on the break and I scored, we got used to playing on the pitch at Hampton Road.

Alan told me about a time when playing for The Racers, lightning hit a tree and struck the pitch, playing at the back so he had a good view. (Lol) Alan Bryan was playing up front, some of the players had to be treated for shock.

Ian Montgomery was John's assistant they were often like chalk and cheese, Monty was a calming influence. John and Monty were a good partnership. On the pitch players like Bobby and Paul Hancock's, George Bryars were solid. (Sinno) Paul Sinnott was strong and reliable, Darren Deeley was very quick. Alan also mentioned Ian Bettles, Craig Dandridge, Gary Hamman all good players.

Thank you for your time Alan, you certainly contributed to the team's great season. In total he made thirty nine appearances scoring two goals.

Craig Dandridge

Craig played in the Central League(Reserves) and Midland Intermediate League for Coventry City. In August 1985 he scored in a 4.1 win for Coventry City reserves over Port Vale. Craig's teammates included Paul Culpin, Graham Rodger, Steve Sedgley, Kirk Stephens and Steve Livingstone.

Ian Bettles

I contacted Ian via Facebook and email and asked him a few questions about his career.

What Junior and senior teams did you play for?

I always played for Long Itchington as a junior. We played in the Leamington League and then the Coventry League. We were very successful. My Dad was again Manager. I joined Racing from Southam United. Deitmar Bruck the Ex Coventry City player was manager for the first couple of seasons and we pottered along mid table. When my Dad took over we also had a couple of average seasons before things started to fall into place.

Your dad as well as being a good manager worked as a scout; did you ever meet any famous players?

My Dad was a football scout first for Leicester City, Coventry City, Middleborough and Swansea. His two biggest finds were David Busst and Shaun Flynn who I both played with.

What are your memories of the 1987/88 championship was it the best team you played in?

The start of the 1987/88 season started with a home draw (I cannot remember the team) and an away draw mid-week against Leamington. We ended up with only 2 points from the first 2 games. I was on holiday for these games and we hadn't played well apparently. We then had a tricky away fixture on the Saturday so we could have ended up with only 2 points from 3 games. Fortunately we won a scrappy game 1-0 and that kick started the season. We then went on an unbelievable run where we dropped very few points. Unfortunately so did Boldmere St Michaels and we were neck and neck going into the last 4 games. If I remember….we also had to play them twice in those 4 games so that would settle the league. The first game at home we drew 0-0 and then we played them mid-week away. I think we won the game 1-2. That left us needing three points from the final two games and those two games was against the bottom of the table team. We won away on the Saturday I think 3-0 so that secured the title and then the home match mid-week was a formality.

This was probably the best team we had. I remember Darren Deeley our leading goal scorer had a brilliant season and scored for fun. But we also were good defensively and had great balance to the team.

Thanks for sharing those memories Ian, In the 1987/88 season he made forty appearances and scored eight goals a very much valued player.

Entertaining Local derby

Racing Club Warwick 2.2 Leamington 27th February 1988 - Midland Combination Premier Division

Darren Deeley scored twice for Racing Club Warwick. Deeley gave the home side the lead then goals from Jawandha and Graham put Leamington in front, Deeley then got the equaliser.

Racing Club Warwick – Hyland, Hannam,Bryars,P Hancocks,Stacey,RHancocks(Shanahan)

Bettles, Dandridge, Sinnott (Coleman) Deeley, White

Leamington - Overton, Myton A, Watkins, Gow, Jawandha, Myton D, Hathaway, Singleton, Harris, Sykes (Price), Graham.

FA Cup run

Racing Club Warwick reached the 3rd qualifying round of the FA Cup, the furthest the club has ever reached.

1987-88	PRE	Oldwinsford	A	1-0
	1Q	Desborough Town	A	2-2
	1Qr	Desborough Town	H	4-0
	2Q	Bedworth United	A	2-1

3Q   Halesowen Town   H   1-3

In the Second Round qualifying match at The Oval, Racing Club Warwick had to come from behind to beat Bedworth United. The Greenbacks took the lead through future Racers manager Dave Draper but hit back through two goals from Paul Sinnott.

Racing Club Warwick 1.3 Halesowen Town – 10th October 1987

Racing Club Warwick welcomed Halesowen to Hampton Road and they gave a good account of themselves against the higher league team. Halesowen scored through Paul Joinson, Lacey and Sherwood with Deeley scoring a well-deserved consolation goal. Halesowen would go onto reach the First Round proper before losing to Kidderminster Harriers after a replay.

Racing Club Warwick – Hyland,P Hancocks,Bryars,R Hancocks,

Shanahan,Stacey,Bettles,Dandridge(Hannam)Sinnott,Deeley,

McKinley(Broad)

Halesowen Town –
Pemberton,Penn,Sherwood,Moore,Lacey.Sturgess,Hancox,

Cunningham,Stringer,P Joinson,L Joinson

The 1990s

Len Derby

I spoke to Len on the phone, he was Racing Club Warwick captain in the early 1990s. Len played football for school team President Kennedy(Coventry) they were unbeaten at home for a number of years. Len won his first trophy with President Kennedy's youth club the Foleshill Charity Shield.

In the late 1970's Len was part of a very successful Sunday League team JF Kennedy Athletic FC. They were first Coventry Sunday Football Club to win the Birmingham County Sunday Junior cup (1975-76). Len played with Shaun McNulty who would play for AP Leamington, Steve Norris who played in the Football League and Ian Crawley who scored the winner for VS Rugby in the 1983 FA Vase final. Sadly Ian passed away in 2008, VS Rugby were managed by Brakes legend Jimmy Knox.

Former AP Leamington players Frank Houston, Tommy Gorman and Danny Conway all played for JF Kennedy Athletic. Len played for AP Leamington in the 1979/80 season playing eight times in the Alliance Premier Division.

AP Leamington v Nuneaton Borough 25-03-1980 Midland Floodlit Cup final first leg

Len played in the first leg which AP Leamington drew 1.1 with Tommy Gorman scoring, they lost the second leg 1.0 Len didn't play in that match.

Leamington: Dulleston, Cooper, D. Taylor, Jones, Brown, Kilkelly, Gorman, M. Taylor, Derby, Gardner, Bain.

Nuneaton Borough: Hall, Stockley, Fallon, Cross, Smithers, Head, Gray, Lang, Neale, Gallagher, Hoult.

Len spent about thirteen years playing for Coventry Sporting, they folded in 1989 he recalls coming back from holiday and receiving a letter about the club folding. After a short break he was contacted by Racing Club Warwick manager John Bettles. In the early 1990s the Racers played in the Southern League Midland Division, Len helped them stay at that level he even scored a winner against Nuneaton Borough in 1991. Racing Club Warwick had a few Coventry Sporting connections back then, goalkeeper

Andy Russell and midfielder Abbey Kelly all played for Sporting. Darren Deeley, Jamie Wootton, Darrell White and Gary Hannam all played with Len at Townsend Meadow.

Len worked with Stuart Dixon a few times, at Racing Club, Wellesbourne and Stratford Town. Towards the end of his playing days he assisted Andy Blair at Racing Club, helping out with the reserves. At Wellesbourne they did well finishing third or fourth in the league.

Len is remembered fondly for his time at Stratford Town under his management they finished in the top six for five consecutive seasons in the early 2000s. Tony Morley the former Aston Villa and England winger, Tranmere Rovers legend Ian Muir and Dennis Bailey the ex Birmingham City and Queens Park Rangers striker and Coventry City's 1987 FA Cup winning midfielder Michael Gynn all played for Stratford in the noughties.

Len praised Martin Sockett he played a big part in the clubs success, Martin was appointed assistant in August 2001.

I asked Len which players stood out in his time in football, Tony Dunk at Coventry Sporting had natural ability. Errington Kelly was a good player, Errington played for AP Leamington he is most remembered for his time with Peterborough United. Leon Woodley, Michael Stephenson and Marcus Hammill were good players.

Len is no longer involved with football he now works in IT, thank you for sharing your memories with me.

Dave Draper

Dave was a successful manager of Racing Club Warwick in the 1990s; I asked him a few questions about his time at the club.

How did the signing of Brian Agar come about? How good was he for you?

At the start of my second season with Racing Club Warwick, I made contact with a few players from Birmingham. Micky Walker, Keith Brown, Mark Smith and Frosty (they had all played for Moor Green) and had decided they wanted to play for a different team.

I was lucky enough to pick them up at the start of the season. Moor Green used to have a formidable strike force of Micky Walker, Brian Agar and Phil Davis. Micky was already with me, Phil remained at Moor Green and whatever I tried he wouldn't move, then there was Brian Agar (aka Bagger).....he was over at Dudley Town. Anyway I didn't really know much about him and I didn't think I need to add as the team had started well and my budget was spent already. We played Dudley away as its happens and he was on the bench ...afterwards his colleagues who were playing for me insisted it would be a good move to put seven days' notice in which I did. The rest is history.....he signed, he kept scoring and we had the most successful season in the club's history. This would not have been the case if I hadn't of signed Brian.

They say management is not about LUCK but it is! if I hadn't have met those boys from Birmingham the high league positions and the two legged final of the Dr Martens Cup v Burton would not have happened.

Do you have a favourite RCW match?

I would be the Dr Martens Cup game away v Merthyr Tydfil.

Here are some of the reasons why

- It was a replayed match as we had gone there the week before only to have it called off for being a frozen pitch.

- It was live on Welsh TV, we won 2.0

- Everyone was introduced on the pitch to the famous ex Juventus player John Charles

- Greg Downs ex Coventry City played at left back for Merthyr Tydfil.

- The coach couldn't get out of the car park because of badly parked cars, so we got out and moved them.

- Brian Agar got to know his future wife, Clare Billington (the chairman's daughter) on that trip.

I was best man!!!

- We went on to beat Worcester City and Ilkeston on our way to the regional Final.

Which players in your time at the club were the most consistent?

Rich Anstiss in goal, Kieran O'Sullivan (captain) and Tony Clarke (right back)

I recently read about an FA Cup match from 1987, you scored for Bedworth against RCW. Do you remember this match?

Yes I remember it well! we (Bedworth) were in the Southern Premier and Warwick was in the Midland Comb, two leagues below. I was from Leamington, Warwick area so I was quite proud to have got to that standard. Then to be beaten by the lads I played Sunday football against (Long Itchington) was a blow. I scored from a header first, while being marked by Alan Stacey.

Jamie Wootton

Jamie was a striker for Racing Club Warwick in the early 1990s, he formed a good partnership with Darren Deeley. I asked Jamie a few questions via Facebook and email.

How did you your career begin, what junior teams did you play for?

I started at Wellesbourne Cubs, then Lighthorne for a season and on to Wellesbourne Junior. Then the men's teams from Stratford league, promoted through all the Coventry leagues. After that the midland Com leagues to the Premier league, winning leagues and lots of cups on the way!!

How long did you play for Wellesbourne for and when did you join RCW?

At twenty one I went to RCW for half a season in the second team then back to Wellesbourne in the Midland Combination. At twenty four Stuart Dixon took me back to RCW in 1990, I started in the reserves then got in the first team. I think I was there for nearly two seasons where in one season I scored seventeen goals in the reserves and sixteen in the first team. Altogether I scored thirty three goals that season.

Did you ever have any trials at any league teams?

No I didn't have any trials, although a Villa scout friend of ours was going to take me but it never happened!

Tell me about the team, what are your memories of playing for RCW?

Darren (Deeley) was my best mate, we were at Kineton High School together. Darren was always the super star and made a lot of my goals!! We had some great players like Lenny Derby, Andy Russell (the goalkeeper) other good players too.

Andy Blair from Villa came in as coach for a while, he is lovely man. My favourite games were Newport County away I scored two. I think the result was 2-2 and the goals were on the telly down there!

Another game was Nuneaton Borough I think it was 3-3. I got one at it was a commentary game on CWR radio

A 2.2 cup game against Hednesford under lights, me and Deeler scored. My goal was a diving header from eighteen yards top corner. Andy Blair said it was the best headed goal he had ever seen!! My first team debut was in the FA Cup against Evesham, great memories!!

Andy Blair one time took me and Deeler up town one night, we were in the back of his car and the back seat collapsed and then the exhaust fell off!! It was hilarious!

I really loved my time there playing in the seventh tier in against players like Frank Worthington, Mark Lawrenson Derek Statham great times!

I also played ten years in the Leamington Sunday League for Wellesbourne it was a really good standard then. All the teams had many players that played at a great Saturday level like Dave Draper Nigel Niblett Casey and Bobby Hancock's. I used to get nearly fifty goals on a Sunday and 30-35 on Saturday football!! We won the Cancer Cup beating Leamington Celtic 3-0! We hammered them and they were the best team then, really good days and great standard! I did my cruciate at twenty seven that was about it then.

Thanks for sharing your memories Jamie.

Brian Agar

One of the best players in local football in the late 1990s and 2000s was Brian Agar.

Brian signed for Leamington in August 2000 he brought valuable experience to the team. In three seasons at the club he made 104 appearances scoring 38 goals.

Millenniums

Into the new century, former Leamington player Steve Sykes was manager of Racing Club Warwick. I asked Steve which were the stand out players in his time at the club. The players were Geoff Amos, Warren Ayers, Simon Windsor and Owen Lovelock.

A line up from December 2000 - Foster, Hodson, Green, Wells, Sidwell, Weston, Holland, Follett, Grey, Eden, Lovelock

At the age of seventeen Ben Foster broke into The Racers first team. Ben would sign for Stoke City in April 2001 and begin his journey to becoming one of the country's best goalkeepers. Racing Club Warwick had some good players back then, Tom Sidwell and Paul (Sniffer) Eden also did well for Leamington.

The Lovelock brothers

Owen Lovelock a defender/midfielder spent time with Stoke City was one of the clubs best players in the early 2000s. Owen also played for Rugby Town and was manager of Stockton FC.

Andy Lovelock a striker who graduated from Lilleshall FA school of excellence he began his career with Coventry City as a trainee. Andy spent time with Crewe Alexandra, Altrincham and Solihull Borough before joining Racing Club Warwick. In April 2004 Andy helped Racing Club Warwick beat local rivals Stratford Town 2.1 at that time he was scoring plenty of goals. Andy up until recently was still scoring goals for Coventry City legends XI's.

Racing Club Warwick were relegated from Southern League Division One West in 2003 after only winning three matches all season. The next season under manager Marcus Law the Racers finished twelfth in the Midland Football Alliance. In the 2003/04 season former Coventry City youth players Tom Cudworth and Gavin O'Toole helped the team to consolidate at their new level. Robert Betts and Dave Titterton who both played for Coventry City's first team played for Racing Club Warwick in the 2000s. A renewed local rivalry in the 2005/06 season when Leamington were promoted from the Midland Combination. The Brakes won both games and finished one place above the Racers in fifth. The next few seasons both clubs fortunes were different, Leamington would win promotions and championships. Racing Club Warwick suffered a bit of a decline from

2009 to 2011 they had three bottom finishes including relegation from The Midland Alliance.

26th December 2005

Racing Club Warwick 0.1 Leamington

Richard Adams scored the only goal of the match which was the first competitive meeting between the neighbours since the 1980s. Both sides included players who played for each side at some point in their career.

Racing Club Warwick Craig Jones; Scott Lower; Nick Green; Robert Betts [Capt.]; Ashley Pringle; Tom Stephenson; Leon Thomas (Jermaine Gordon); Darren Beckett (Mark Faulds); James Wood (Ben Mackie); Paul White; Ollie Olanipekun

Leamington Richard Morris; Jon Adams; Darran Tank; Ryan Parisi; Neil Stacey; Morton Titterton; Stuart Herlihy; Leon Morgan [Capt.]; Richard Adams (Paul Eden); Ryan Howell (Martin Thompson); Josh Blake

Current team

Racing Club Warwick currently competes in the Midland League Premier Division having won promotion from the Midland Football League Division One in the 2018/19 season.

The 2018/19 season will be remembered for years to come at Townsend Meadow, Manager Scott Easterlow appointed in May 2017 achieved promotion in two years. Scott had been successful in his three years with Stockton guiding them to promotion to the top level of the Coventry Alliance. As a player he turned out for Racing Club Warwick , Alveston, Leamington, Rugby Town, Coventry Copsewood and Kenilworth Town. The star of the team was former Coventry City and Leamington striker

Ben(Magic)Mackey who scored thirty seven goals. Although Ben grabbed the headlines with his goals it is a collective effort, players like Charlie Bannister, Joe Smith, Scott Turner and Luke Cole to name a few were all consistent. Scott's assistant / goalkeeping coach Neil Stacey is available as a back-up keeper he also plays outfield for Westlea Wanderers on a Sunday.

Memorable match

8th October 2018

Racing Club Warwick 2.1 Heather St Johns

Racers end visitor's unbeaten start to the season and show there promotion credentials with this good home win. Gardner scored for Heather then Ben Mackey got a brace to seal the points for Racing Club Warwick. Heather St Johns would go onto win the league with Racing Club finishing second to achieve promotion.

Racing Club Warwick –
Bannister,Passey,Powell,Castleton,Turner,Smith,Leaver,Price(Quartermaine) Mackey,Malley(Billington)Jeys

A new season and marque signing

On the 13th June 2019, Racing Club Warwick announced that they have signed midfielder Kevin Thornton. Kev was born in Drogheda , Ireland on 9th July 1986 an attacking midfielder he came through the youth team at Coventry City making his first team debut on 20 September 2005. Kev's first appearance was as an eighty third minute substitute in a League Cup tie against Crystal Palace which Sky Blues lost one nil, maybe if he had come on earlier the result may have been different. In his brief cameo he took the game to Palace, Coventry pressed for the equaliser but The Eagles held on. Coventry fans were impressed with his performance and he was pushing for a first team starting place. Kev made fifty five first team appearances scoring two goals including the winner against Hull City on the 26th August 2006, his time at the Ricoh he was mainly used as an impact player from the bench. Chris Coleman gave Kev a run in the team when he took over as manager in February 2008, Kev played well with Jay Tabb. Jay praised him he said he was revelling in his central midfield role. The 2008/09 he spent time on loan at Brighton and Hove Albion, only playing five times that season for Coventry City. In July 2009 Kev left Coventry City by mutual consent for disciplinary issues, he played briefly for Coventry Sphinx, Irish team Boyne Rovers FC and Nuneaton Town before signing for League Two team Northampton Town in January 2010.

Cobbler's boss Ian Sampson signed Kev after impressing on trial, his most memorable match would have to be on 22nd September 2010 when Northampton Town caused a major upset by knocking Liverpool out of the Carling Cup at Anfield. Liverpool fielded a so called weaker team but still included internationals Lucas, Babel, Agger. The Reds took the lead through Jovanovic, Cobblers equalised through McKay which meant the scores were level after ninety minutes. Jacobs gave Northampton the lead in extra time only for Ngog to level, Kev had assisted in both of the Cobblers goals. Neither side could find a winner so it went to penalties which Northampton won by four goals to two. A famous win for Northampton and possibly one of Kevin Thornton's best of his career.

Liverpool

Jones ,Agger ,Kyrgiakos ,Wilson ,Kelly, Lucas, Spearing, Pacheco (Ince), Jovanovic (Eccleston)

Babel (Shelvey), Ngog

Northampton Town

Dunn, Rodgers (Herbert) Johnson (Wedderburn) Tozer, Thornton, Gilligan, Osman, Holt, Jacobs,

Davis, McKay (Guinan)

In the summer of 2011 he was given a month-by-moth contact he was released in September 2011 making forty five appearances in total. A second spell with Nuneaton followed but appearances were restricted by injury he then joined Wrexham after a trial. Kev scored a penalty for Wrexham in their FA Trophy victory in 2013 he was substituted for current Brakes midfielder Joe Clarke on eight nine minutes.

A loan spell at Tamworth was followed by a permanent move, Kev played for The Lambs in the 2014/15 season. The next few seasons would see him at Rugby Town, Barwell, Coventry United and AFC Hinckley.

Kev has made a good start to his time with The Racers, he scored a penalty against his old team Coventry United in October 2019. Still only thirty three hopefully he stay at the club and help them achieve another promotion he seems to be enjoying his football I wish him and Racing Club Warwick all the very best for the rest of the season.

Chapter Ten – Irish players in Leamington and Warwick

In the 1950s Irishmen Hugh Morrow and Eddie O'Hara both played for Lockheed Leamington. Hugh also played for Northampton Town and West Bromwich Albion. Eddie also played league football for Birmingham City.

Footballers from Ireland were very prominent in local football in the 1960s and 1970s. Tommy Gorman, Tom Kilkelly and Frank Houston were all good players for AP Leamington in the late 1970s.

Tom Lewin

I asked Tom Lewin if he could tell me about the best Irish players he remembers.

Leamington has a great tradition for Irish people, a lot due to the closure of Fords in Cork. Workers were offered employment in Ford factories across the UK such as Leamington.

Whittle Wanderers began with a good Irish contingent and continued that way. We had two Irish managers, Jerome Buckley and Johnny O'Sullivan, characters both of them...

Players over the years who played for Whittle Wanderers with Irish connections...

Condon brothers - John, Billy and Jamey and O'Connor brothers - Tim, Alex, Anthony and Willie. Paddy Taylor, Dony Shanahan , Ollie Guinane, John Cunningham, Tucker & John O'Callaghan , Paddy & Don Hill . Liam & Eddie Fitzpatrick, Don Murphy , Tom O'Reilly, Paddy Crowley , Mick

& Pete Murphy , Glenn Cleary , Gary O'Brian , Martin O'Regan, Frank & Noel Daly .Sean McFarlane...I am sure I missed a few...

Two players that stood out in our 1969/70 season were Martin Doyle and John Kinsella these two lads came from Dublin. Martin Doyle was a prodigious footballer, I rated him as one of Whittle's best ever players a midfielder with incredible ball control who scored over twenty five goals in that season.

He had one flaw which was his self-control; he was subjected to some ruthless tackles by opposing teams. Martin was sent off on two occasions, retaliation, once for us and once for his Saturday team, Leamington Celtic. How about this, he was selected to play for the 'Leamington Select' and was unable to play because he was suspended! And at the time Whittle Wanderers were a Division Three team. Martin and John went back to Dublin after just one year in Leamington, often wondered how they got on...

Other Irish players in Leamington include - Paddy & John Caden, Billy Shanahan, John O'Kelly, Chrissy Henderson, Shifty Burke, Tommy O'Connor, Shay Thurlow, Ted Forde, Finbar Keane, and Liam Fitzgerald Dennis Long.

Paddy Crowley

One of the best Irish players in local football in the 1970s, I asked Paddy a few questions via Facebook.

Could you tell me what Junior and senior teams you played for?

I was born in Cork City Ireland 1953. My first adult Sunday team was Spa Rangers then Radford United. I then played for Leamington Celtic and Whittle Wanderers.

My first Saturday clubs were .Bishop's Tachbrook AP Works .Kineton United. Radford United. Teammates included -Johnny Bull, Ollie Guinane, Alan Bryan, Mick and Pete Murphy, Brian Mathews and Bob Ballantyne...

You were part of a good Leamington Celtic team have you Irish heritage, some great Irish players in the 1970s?

My Celtic teammates included -Denis Long, Tony Murray, Tony O'Conner, Pat Callaghan, Mick Murphy and Liam Fitzgerald.

Who were the toughest players you played against?

Toughest players were - Roger Constable, Alan Stacey, Dave Mc Mahon, Ian Walker (RIP) and Steve Cooper.

Jim Barry

Jim was originally from Cork in Ireland, Jim moved to Leamington in search of work. A keen footballer whose preferred position was left half played football for Improved Hinges, Warwick Central, Cubbington Albion, Saltisford Rovers, Leamington Celtic and Leamington Postal.

A good player in his day he scored a great goal on 14th April 1962 Jim for Saltisford Rovers against Stratford Town a shot from an acute angle on the left wing.

In April 1965 when Jim was playing for Saltisford Rovers he captained a Warwickshire Combination XI to play against a South Essex Football League XI. The team also included local players Smith (Saltisford Rovers) Johnson (Warwick Town) and Keenan (Stratford Town)

In 1974, along with wife Joy, Jim set up Leamington Hibernians on Bury Road in the town. They have gone on to become an established football club with teams in different age groups. To this day Jim and Joy are still involved with the club. Jim won an award from the FA in 2011 for his services to local football which is truly deserved.

Jim has a famous aunty Kathy Barry who is famous in the city of Cork. Barry was a well-known figure around the city in the 1950s and 1960s, running a síbín and 'eating house' on Cornmarket St (Coal Quay) which is an area of Cork famous for its street traders. In September 2019 Cork City Hall were considering the possibility of erecting a statue of Kathy who passed away in 1982.

I got in touch with Siobhàn Gordon who is Jim's daughter. Siobhan kindly told me about Jim's life in football.

Dad got into football many years ago in Cork City where he was brought up in Gurranabraher and attended Blarney Street School. Jim played Hurling and Gaelic Football and his Dad John started a football team called Red City (named after the colour of the roof tiles in the newly built Gurranabraher). Jim played for Red City's U14 team at the age of nine years old ,and he continued to play for Red City growing up. Jim was showing great promise as a footballer and scouts were watching him, however, Jim was taken into Dublin hospital aged thirteen for radiation treatment. This was used to treat the inflammation of the spine in patients with ankylosing spondylitis. After treatment Jim was told he'd never play football again!

As with most young men in the 1950's Jim has to move to Leamington Spa for work. Jim played for the following teams; St Peters Celtic, Improved Hinges (Warwick Men's), Warwick Central U21, Satisford Rovers (where he never took the wage packet), Cubbington Albion, and Leamington Celtic where Jim was a player and manager. In fact Jim was the manager when Tommy Doherty brought Glasgow Celtic under 16's to Edmondscote Track for a friendly. Unlike many of the other Irish men that moved to Leamington, Jim did not work at the Fords Factory. Jim did go there for a job but they said he was too small!! There were many notable matches over the years at all Levels but one that stands out was when Leamington Hibs U13's played the Bradberry Boys in the Mid Warwickshire Boys League final at the Windmill Ground. A great match which Hibs won 5-3, many great young up and coming players were in that team (Jim doesn't like to be backed in a corner re who were the best but says they all had something to bring to the field that day). Jim loves to reminisce about all the players and matches and refers to Malcolm McGreevey as they most gifted and skilful player he ever say in Leamington. Jim still runs Leamington Hibs Saturday men's team who play in the Midland League Division Three and his wife Joy still by his side each Saturday.

Jim founded Leamington Hibernians to ensure that every child in Leamington had a chance to have a game of football regardless of their background. It really didn't matter if a child couldn't pay their

subscriptions as Jim would cover it himself. As long as the child got a game, enjoyed themselves and learnt, that's what made it all very much worthwhile.

Jim refused to ever take money for a game of football. Jim was never ever booked in all the years he played football. Jim's wedding was moved to closed season by his priest after Jim asked if he could squeeze a match in between the wedding service and the reception!

Jim's son Kevin was a top goal scorer for Mid Warwickshire Boys. Kevin's brother Liam was a hard working footballer who once scored one of the best goals Jim ever saw. Siobhan told me that Tony Anderson was an excellent player, Tony played in the same team as Kevin.

Leamington Spa's first Republic of Ireland International

Jordan Shipley was born in Leamington in 1997 and he attended Trinity Catholic School. A promising young midfielder, Jordan came through the youth team at Coventry City establishing himself in the first team in the 2017/18. Jordan's form earned him a call up to Republic of Ireland Under 21 team in October 2018. In May 2018 he scored Coventry City's second goal in the League Two play off final win over Exeter City. Jordan's goal in that match made him the first Leamington born player to score at Wembley Stadium. Jordan has continued to develop and has flourished playing in an advance role in Coventry City's push for promotion this season. If Sky Blues do achieve promotion to the Championship surely it can't be long before Mick McCarthy calls Jordan up to Ireland's senior squad. Still only twenty two If Jordan continues to progress he should become a regular for club and country.

Leamington FC Irish internationals

Michael Quirke

A goalkeeper who made four appearances for Coventry City FC in the Championship. Michael made his debut on 14th August 2010 in a 2.2 draw v Watford, coming on a substitute for the injured Iain Turner. In March 2011 Michael made his debut for Republic of Ireland under 21 against Portugal. Michael was briefly at Leamington in 2012 also had spells with Nuneaton Borough, Bedworth United and Kettering Town. Now at the age of twenty eight he plays as a defender for Coventry United he is also captain.

Darren Stableton

A defender/ midfielder who made five appearances for Leamington FC in the 2010/11 season. Darren played in Ireland for Kildare County, Dundalk and Shamrock Rovers he also had spells with Reading and Solihull Moors. Darren has represented Republic of Ireland at under 16, 17, 18, 19 and 21 levels.

Cieron Keane

A defender who played has spent time with Wolverhampton Wanderers and Notts County. Cieron played a couple of times for The Magpies before signing for Nuneaton Town in 2015 then played for a few non-league teams including Worcester City and Kidderminster Harriers. In 2019 he joined Leamington and has since joined Bradford Park Avenue. Cieron played for Republic of Ireland under 19s in 2014.

Chapter Eleven- Kenilworth

Over the years Kenilworth has produced some fine players who have played at the very top level of English football and represented the national team. We are going to look at a few players and managers who are from or have lived in the town.

George Hollis

George was born in Kenilworth in 1869 he was a goalkeeper for Small Heath between 1891 and 1894. Small Heath would become Birmingham City, George played forty nine times for the club winning the Football League Second Division in 1892/93. Whilst at Small Heath he deputised for Chris Charsley who became the first player from the club to play for England. George later played for Bournbrook FC, Not much is known about his life outside football.

John Walter Jarvis

Born in Kenilworth in 1888, a centre forward who played once for Coventry City in the 1912/13 Southern League season. John also played for Longford St Thomas, Hawkesbury FC, Kenilworth Town and Nuneaton Town.

Barry Powell

Born in Kenilworth In January 1954, he lived in Mortimer Road in the town. In 1967 a thirteen year old Barry was captain of Castle High School and St John's Boys Club, a promising young player who had been watched by Stoke City. He signed forms with the Potters who then have the option on him when he is fifteen.

In January 1972 an eighteen year old Barry signed as a professional for Wolverhampton Wanderers. Barry made his Wolves debut on the 10th of March 1973 in a 1.1 draw against Crystal Palace. The next two years he featured on a regular basis for Wolves including an appearance in the

League Cup Final on 2nd March 1974 as an 83rd minute substitute. Wolves beat a talented Manchester City 2.1 thanks to goals from Kenny Hibbitt and John Richards, Colin Bell scoring for City. Manchester City's front five were Bell, Law, Lee, Summerbee and Marsh; however Wolves had a good blend of experience in Bailey, Dougan and youth in Powell and Sunderland. A Leamington connection in the Wolves team Geoff Palmer's son Steve played for the Brakes in 2009. 1974 was a great year for Barry, winning a trophy at Wembley and playing for England at Under 23 level, quite possibly the first Kenilworth lad to do both. Whilst playing for his country he played with some very good players – Steve Perryman, Dennis Tueart and Bob Latchford.

Barry played in the North American Soccer League for Portland Timbers in the summer of 1975. In September 1975 Barry signed for Coventry City with Willie Carr going to Wolves, Barry made his debut for The Sky Blues on 10th September 1975 against Bolton Wanderers in the League Cup. In his early days at Highfield Road he played briefly with Dennis Mortimer, Barry scored at Anfield in a fine 1.1 draw against Liverpool in November 1975. Coventry fans were outraged when Mortimer was sold to Aston Villa but with Barry they had a player who was a capable replacement. Barry often played alongside John Craven in midfield for the rest of the 1975/76 season. It wasn't until Welsh international Terry Yorath arrived at Highfield Road in 1976 did Barry flourish in midfield. Barry established himself as an attacking midfielder with a strong shot who scored plenty of goals. The 1977/78 season was one of Coventry City's best ever seasons finishing seventh in the First Division. Powell and Yorath in the engine room with wing wizard Tommy Hutchison, prolific strikers Ian Wallace and Mick Ferguson. Barry signed for Derby County in 1979 then had spells with Burnley, Swansea City, USA, and Hong Kong before returning to Wolves for a short spell in November 1986. After finishing playing Barry worked for Coventry City in football in the community scheme and he managed Hednesford Town and Aberystwyth Town.

I contacted Barry by Facebook and asked him a couple of questions.

Do you regret not playing international football for Wales?

I got selected to play for England youth v Scotland at Villa Park, I was sub and got on for 10 mins. When my career started to take off Wales called the English FA to see if they had any problems with selecting me for an u23 international against England, the reply was yes go ahead and play him. Sir Alf Ramsey came to watch me play for Wolves; he then pulled me out of the Welsh team and put me in the English team for the same game by virtue of me playing for England in the youth international against Scotland for 10 mins. I was then selected to play in the same game for England against Wales.

Did you dad play for Kenilworth Rangers?

Yes he did, my Dad played for Warwick Town too, and He was at Cardiff as a kid and was on his way to QPR when he had the accident that prevented him from playing as a professional.

Memorable match

Coventry City 5.1 Chelsea – 14th January 1978 League Division One

Sky Blues demolished Chelsea at Highfield Road, Leamington lad Mick Coop scored a penalty then two goals from Ray Graydon, One each for Bobby McDonald and Ian Wallace. Barry Powell and Terry Yorath getting the better of Ray Wilkins and Ray Lewington in midfield. Wilkins got Chelsea's goal.

Coventry City – Blyth, Coop, McDonald, Osgood, Roberts, Yorath, Powell, Graydon, Hutchison, Ferguson, Wallace

Chelsea – Bonetti, Harris, Wicks, Britton, Graham Wilkins, Sparrow, Lewington, Walker, Ray Wilkins, Garner, Langley

Barry is certainly one of Warwickshire's best ever footballers who is a Wolves and Coventry City legend.

Bob Steane

A Kenilworth kid, Bob was a talented goalkeeper who began playing for local side Abbey Rangers in 1962 he also played for Aston Villa and

Walsall's A teams then Stratford Town, Nuneaton Borough, Warley and Kenilworth Rangers. In 1968 whilst playing for Kenilworth Rangers he was approached by Lockheed Leamington then managed by Sid Ottewell. The Brakes also had another talented local goalkeeper Tony Partridge on their books. The highlight of Bob's time with Lockheed was winning the Birmingham Senior Cup in 1970 beating Burton Albion in the final. Bob was released by Jimmy Knox in 1973 after five seasons with the club. Bob played a couple of years for Leamington Sunday League team Whittle Wanderers.

Bob attended Warwick School he was a fine cricketer an opening batsman and medium paced seam bowler. He also represented Leamington and Warwick Cricket Club's. Bob sadly passed away in 2011 aged sixty three. There is a nice interview on the Brakes trust website in which Bob talks about playing against Ivor Allchurch, Ron Flowers and Eddy Clamp. His joy of winning the Senior Cup and the memorable performance in the semi-final, also his sadness at being released by Lockheed.

Tim Flowers

Born in Kenilworth on the 3rd of February 1967, Tim went to Park Hill School and Kenilworth Comprehensive. During his school days Tim was in the same year as Graham Rodger, Graham was born in Scotland but grew up in Kenilworth. Both players were at Wolverhampton Wanderers the same time. Tim and Graham were both scouted by John Hannah. The year above them was Graham Clutton who played for AP Leamington. Tim broke into the Wolves team aged eighteen, however it was a bleak time for the club as they suffered successive relegations. Within two years from 1984 to 1986 Wolves went from the First Division to the Fourth Division. A teammate of both Tim and Graham at Molineux was former AP Leamington star Mark Buckland. Tim is no relation to 1960s Wolves legend Ron Flowers.

Tim represented England at Under 16, 18 and 21 levels, playing alongside future England teammates Tony Adams and Paul Gascoigne.

11th June 1987

France 2.0 England – Toulon under 21 tournament

Kenilworth lads Tim Flowers and Graham Rodger both played in the same England under 21 team. France won this game thanks to goals from Lambert and Ginola (yes David) a proud day for Park Hill Primary School and the town of Kenilworth. Graham had won an FA Cup winners medal a month before, Coventry City teammate Steve Sedgley also played in this match.

England –

Flowers,Caeser,Dorigo,Gibbs,Rodger,Brennan(Sedgley)Dozzell,Gordon,Porter,Simpson,

Rosario (Clough)

Tim joined Southampton in 1986 as an understudy to Peter Shilton, he made a few appearances for The Saints plus a loan spell at Swindon Town. By the 1989/90 season Tim was first choice goalkeeper and was getting a reputation of one of the country's best keepers. 1993 Tim was at his peak and he finally made his England debut against Brazil on the 13th of June in the US Cup the match ended 1.1. In November 1993 he joined Blackburn Rovers for £2.4 million which made him the most expensive goalkeeper in Britain. Tim stayed at Ewood Park for six years, in 1995 Blackburn Rovers won the Premiership then Tim played in the Champions League. In 2000 he won the League Cup with Leicester City and finished his playing career with spells at Stockport County, Coventry City and Manchester City. Tim went into coaching and was assistant manager under Iain Dowie at Coventry City in 2007 for a year. Tim worked at various clubs including Queens Park Rangers, Hull City, Northampton Town and Nottingham Forest, recently manager of Solihull Moors in the National League. Tim guided the team to a good FA Cup run and a promotion challenge in the 2018/19 season. At the time of writing, Tim and Solihull Moors parted company by mutual consent, with the team occupying eighth position in the National League. Out of 92 games in charge he won 44 and lost 25, not a bad ratio. One of Warwickshire's greatest players, I wish Tim the very best in his next challenge.

Simon Rea

Simon was born in Kenilworth on the 20th September 1976, a central defender who played in the Football League for Birmingham City and Peterborough United. I spoke to Simon on the phone and asked him a few questions about his football career. Simon now lives in Leamington and is married into a very fine football family his wife Lisa is Ian and Chris Walkers daughter.

Simon like Tim Flowers and Graham Rodger is a former pupil of Park Hill School in Kenilworth, the school must be so proud to have them as former pupils.

A talented player as a kid, at the age of fourteen Simon represented Warwickshire schools and signed schoolboy forms for Division Three side Birmingham City. Simon was a versatile player who play either centre half or centre forward, at this could time he attended Kenilworth school and captained Mid-Warwickshire schools. He also played for Norton Lindsay who were top of the under 14 Central Warwickshire League, Simon previously played for Coten End Colts.

Simon made his first team debut for Birmingham City up front in the 1995/96 season; he played in central defence for the youth team and scored twenty seven goals! This led him to play for the reserves up front. In total he played two matches for The Blues first team against Leicester City in the league and v Genoa in the Anglo-Italian Cup. In the mid-1990s Birmingham City had some very good defenders like Michael Johnson, Gary Breen, Steve Bruce and Gary Ablett so Simon's first team chances were very limited, Simon told me he probably stayed at Birmingham too long, but it would have been good to learn of players who have played at the very top level of English football. Steve Finnan was also at St Andrews at the same time both young players, he made more appearances than Simon but left in March 1996. Steve went onto have a great career with Fulham, Liverpool and Republic Of Ireland. Simon was at Birmingham

City under a few managers from Terry Cooper, Barry Fry and Trevor Francis,

Simon joined Peterborough United in 1999 reuniting him with Barry Fry; he would become a fans favourite in his six years at London Road. He spoke fondly of his time at Peterborough, Jimmy Bullard, Leon McKenzie and Steve Castle stood out. Simon remembers the FA Cup match against Newcastle United in January 2002, Peterborough had a good go and twice come from behind to level. It would be Alan Shearer and co who would get two late goals, Simon said that it was hard playing against Craig Bellamy he was so tricky had some much pace. One of the best players he faced in the league was Jermaine Defoe who was on loan at AFC Bournemouth. Barry Fry is still at Peterborough now as director of football, as a manager Barry liked to sign players who he managed previously; Simon, Andy Edwards and Steve Castle were at Birmingham City when he was boss. I remember seeing Simon play in an FA Cup match at Highfield Road in 2003 for a couple of seasons in a row both teams played each other in cup competitions.

Memorable match

Peterborough United 1.0 Darlington – 26th May 2000 Third Division play-off final –Wembley

In one of the last ever matches at the Old Wembley, Peterborough won promotion thanks to a goal from former Wimbledon striker Andy Clarke. Darlington was the better team in the first half they had decent players like former Sunderland striker Marco Gabbiadini, but Posh defended well. Simon Rea put a superb battling defensive display to keep a clean sheet. Peterborough had sold star players Simon Davies and Matthew Etherington half way through the season so credit to the team for carrying on and winning promotion.

Peterborough United: Mark Tyler, Richard Scott, Adam Drury, Simon Rea, Andy Edwards, Jon Cullen, Steve Castle, David Farrell, Gareth Jelleyman, David Oldfield, Andy Clarke.

Darlington: Andy Collett, Paul Heckingbottom, Steve Tutill, Michael Oliver, Neil Aspin, Craig Liddle, Martin Gray, Brian Atkinson, Marco Gabbiadini, Peter Duffield, Neil Heaney.

After Simon left Peterborough in 2005 he dropped into Non-league football with Nuneaton Borough, Kidderminster Harriers, Redditch United and Leamington. By 2006/2007 Simon finished playing, unfortunately injuries prevented him playing professionally so he studied for a Sports Science Degree. Simon played one match for Leamington in September 2008 against Studley in the Birmingham Senior Cup; he helped out at Whitnash coaching. Simon's son is now on Birmingham City's books maybe one day he could follow in his dad's footsteps and become a professional footballer.

Thank you so much for your time Simon; it has been a pleasure being able to include you in my book.

Dave Sexton

A successful club and international manager who was a resident of Kenilworth for over thirty years. Dave Sexton was born in Islington, London on the 6th of April 1930 the son of professional boxer Archie Sexton.

Dave played mainly as an inside forward beginning his career at non-league teams Newmarket Town and Chelmsford City before signing professional for Luton Town in 1951. A good career in the 1950s playing for West Ham United alongside future managers Malcolm Allison, Noel Cantwell and Frank O'Farrell. Dave also played for Leyton Orient, Brighton and Hove Albion and Crystal Palace, he won the Third Division (South) with Brighton. At The Boleyn Ground, Dave had a good goal scoring record of 29 goals in 77 appearances. Cartilage problems saw him finish his playing a couple of months before his 30th birthday.

In February 1962 Dave became assistant coach at Chelsea under Tommy Docherty; ironically he would replace Docherty as manager in 1967 after spells at Leyton Orient, Fulham and Arsenal. Dave spent seven years at Stamford Bridge he enjoyed goo d success with The Blues winning the FA

Cup and European Cup Winners Cup. The late 1960s and early 1970s was a great era for Chelsea with club legends Ron Harris, Charlie Cooke, Peter Bonetti, Alan Hudson and Peter Osgood in the team. Towards the end of Dave's time as manager, the club had financial problems combined with disputes with fans favourites he was sacked in October 1974.

Dave didn't have to wait long for another job, he was appointed as manager of Queen's Park Rangers. The mid-1970s was a golden era at Loftus Road, the greatest team in the clubs history. Dave was so very close in leading QPR to the First Division title in the 1975/76 only pipped by Liverpool by one point!

Dave built an exciting squad of players including the Maverick Stan Bowles who should have won a lot more England caps. David Webb and John Hollins had played for Dave previously at Chelsea. Gerry Francis was England captain and a driving force in midfield. Frank McLintock, Don Masson, Don Givens, Dave Thomas, Phil Parkes, Ian Gillard and Dave Clement were all quality players. The QPR team of the 1975/76 is often regarded as one of the best teams never to win the league.

In the summer of 1977 Dave replaced Tommy Docherty as manager again, this time at Manchester United. High profile signings Gordon McQueen, Joe Jordan, Ray Wilkins and Gary Birtles plus established players Steve Coppell, Lou Macari and Gordon Hill, Dave had talented players at the club however they never won a trophy. United were runners up in the league and FA Cup, but a club that size wants trophies which meant Dave was sacked in 1981.

In May 1981 Dave took over from Gordon Milne as manager of Coventry City. The Sky Blues had an exciting young team in the early 1980s they reached the League Cup semi-final in the 1980/81 season. Dave signed his ex-captain Gerry Francis although coming to the end of his career added valuable experience. Mark Hateley, Danny Thomas and Gary Gillespie would all become full international players, Garry Thompson, Paul Dyson and Steve Whitton all had decent careers. Ironically Dave's first match was against Manchester United which Coventry City won 2.1 thanks to goals from Bodak and Whitton, Macari scored for United. During his two seasons at Highfield Road the Sky Blues enjoyed good home form which kept them in the division. Coventry only just avoided relegation in the 1982/83 season it coincided with the sale of striker Garry Thompson who was sold without Dave's knowledge, some would say the writing was on the wall as he was sacked at the end of the season.

Success with England

Dave was England under 21 head coach/manager from 1977 to 1990 and later between 1994 and 1996. The glory years were in 1982 and 1984 when Dave led England to the European Under-21 Championship. Both finals were played over two legs

1982

Gary Owen and Justin Fashanu's goals in the first leg gave England a cushion for the second leg in West Germany. Rudi Voller and Pierre Littbarski were the outstanding players of the tournament and would go onto bigger and greater things, but England did enough over two legs to win the trophy for the first time.

England 3-1 West Germany
(Owen 2 Fashanu, Völler)

West Germany 3-2 England
(Littbarski 3 Duxbury, Goddard)
(agg: 5-4 to England)

1984

England beat a Spanish side over two legs that included future internationals goalkeeper Andoni Zubizarreta, prolific striker Emilio Butragueno and Real Madrid midfielder Michel. The tournament's top scorer was England's Mark Hateley who Dave had managed at Coventry City; Mark would soon make a dream move to AC Milan.

Spain 0.1 England

Sterland

England 2.0 Spain

Hateley, Gayle

Dave was also England assistant manager and he also became Technical Director at the FA's National School at Lilleshall. In 2005 he was awarded the OBE for his services to football.

In 2008 Sexton House in Talisman Square in Kenilworth was named in his honour. Dave lived in Kenilworth since the early 1980s when he became manager of Coventry City. Dave sadly passed away in 2012 at the age of 82 his funeral took place at St Francis of Assisi Catholic Church in Kenilworth.

The People of Kenilworth can be very proud of Dave; he's up there with the best coaches this country has produced.

Kenilworth football clubs

Kenilworth Rangers were a successful side in the late 1940s and early 1950s. In 1992 they changed their name to Kenilworth Town. In the 1995-96 season they were Midland Combination Division One runners up only by goal difference of two goals however they were promoted to Premier Division. In 1993 and 1996 Kenilworth Town won the Saturday Challenge Vase.

Kenilworth Rangers glory days

8th April 1949

Kenilworth Rangers score nine goals

Kenilworth beat Lockheed reserves by nine goals to nil; Jones scored three and two each for Samwell and Watts. Walker and Swann completed the scoring for Rangers. Kenilworth goalkeeper was once on the books of Coventry City but he never played for the first team.

Kenilworth Rangers – Halliwell, Shaw, Murray, J Bostock, R Bostock, Routledge, Swann, Watts, Jones, Walker, Samwell

1st May 1951

Telegraph Cup for Kenilworth

Kenilworth Rangers beat Brico 3.2 to win the Evening Telegraph Challenge Cup at Highfield Road. This is the first time that Rangers have won this cup. Kenilworth goals were scored by Collett, Jones and Bostock.

Kenilworth Rangers – Clarke, Cardner, Truelove, J Bostock, R Bostock, Routledge, Collett, Watts, Jones, Warren, Samwell

21st September 1951

Kenilworth players in County team

Kenilworth Rangers half back Routledge and centre forward Jones have been selected to play for Birmingham County FA team against Staffordshire. A Southern Amateur championship match, Jones recently scored six goals against Morris Motors in a Coventry and North Warwickshire League game.

24th April 1954

Kenilworth and Standard share cup

Kenilworth Rangers and Standard Athletic agreed to become joint holders of the Coventry Charity Cup after the final at the Butts Stadium was abandoned due to bad light. At full time the score was 0.0 so they decided to play extra time however it became obvious that the light would not last. After a consultation with both teams' secretaries it was decided that they would share the cup.

16th September 1960

Kenilworth Rangers open new ground

Kenilworth are to play Cubbington in a Warwickshire Combination match at their new ground at Thickthorn. The ground is adjacent to Kenilworth Rugby Football Club on Glasshouse Lane, Previously Rangers played on Scots Road which is now being built on. Kenilworth's old ground on Scots Road is now occupied by The Gauntlet pub and Oaks shopping precinct.

13th April 1965

Kenilworth late goal wins cup

Kenilworth Rangers won the Coventry Benevolent Cup beating Coventry Hood and Sidescreen 2.1. Evans and Murphy scored Ranger's goals.

9th April 1966

Kenilworth Rangers take Foleshill Cup

Kenilworth Rangers beat Standard Athletic 1.0 at the Morris Motors ground in Courthouse Green to win the Foleshill Charity Cup. Outside right John McGowan scored the winning goal.

Paul Barnett

Paul played was a striker for Kenilworth Rangers for four years in the 1970s. Paul sadly passed away in 2015 aged sixty one. I contacted Paul's daughter Donna and asked her a few questions about her dad's career.

What other teams your dad played for?

Lutterworth Town Coventry Telegraph team and Kenilworth working men's club

Did your dad have any trials at any professional clubs?

Yes Wolverhampton Wanderers, He had a few trial games.

Paul in the news

24th September 1977

Rangers progress in Birmingham Junior Cup

Paul Barnett scored a fine goal from thirty five yards, He then won a penalty which Hackleton converted. Brady completed the scoring.

Kenilworth Rangers – Ray Young, Rob Young, Howell, Jones, Bennett, Clarke, McStay, Taylor, Hackleton,

Barnett, Brady

21st January 1978

Paul Barnett in prolific form for Kenilworth WMC

Kenilworth WMC are having a great season in the Coventry & District League and recently beat Reynold Chain 7.3 in the Sheet Metal Fabricators Cup. Paul Barnett scored a couple of goals to take his total for the season to thirty seven, Jim O'Malley and Dave Worrall also scored.

23rd December 1978

Hat-rick for Barnett

Paul Barnett scored three goals for Kenilworth Rangers as they hammered Wolston in a Coventry and North Warwickshire Premier Division game/

Mick Burke

Mick as a player and manager was a stalwart for Kenilworth Rangers. I contacted his son Sean to ask him a few questions about his dad's career.

How long was he Kenilworth Rangers manager for?

He managed Kenilworth Rangers first team from 1979 to 2002 then he stopped and went to Sunday league 2003 to 2006 with the Gauntlet football team

From 2009 to 2015 my dad helped me be involved with kind of town reserves and in 2014 I took over from my dad so I looked after Kenilworth Town Reserves for 2 1/2 seasons and then went back to went back to play rugby

Could you ask him if he has any favourite matches for Rangers?

His most favourite moment was when he won when the team won the Coventry Charity Cup. Mick's favourite player was Jim O'Malley.

Do you play football yourself Sean?

I played for Kenilworth Town Reserves and I also played in the Sunday League for Kenilworth Town

Both Mick and Sean played cricket for Kenilworth and Leek Wooton.

Dave Shilton

Dave is very well known in Kenilworth for his work in the community and the council. Dave has been Town Mayor Twice and also been Chairman of Warwick District and Warwickshire County Councils. Originally from Baddesley Ensor in North Warwickshire he moved to Kenilworth at a young age. Dave played football for St John's School and St Nicholas Schools in Kenilworth and was selected to play for Warwickshire. A right winger very fast who scored plenty of goals his nickname was sniffer.

Dave was part of a strong Kenilworth WMC team in the 1970s that included many local players who also played for Kenilworth Rangers. Jim O'Malley was the pick of the players Dave recalls "Jim was good enough to play at a higher level a midfield play maker"

"Barry Jones was a good centre forward, Paul Barnett a great player fantastic with free kicks" Dave also talked about Keith Bennett (full back) Robin Burke (Goalkeeper) and Steve Flowers who was on the books of Aston Villa. Brian and Steve Flowers were cousins of professional goalkeeper Tim Flowers.

Back in the 1960s and 1970s they used Abbey Fields to play both Saturday and Sunday football. Dave also played for Arden Products and Stoneleigh, he recalls playing against the good teams of Leamington back in those days.

Thanks for your time Dave, great to speak to you.

Bryan Flowers

I asked Bryan a few questions about his playing career.

What position did you play? How long did you play for Kenilworth Rangers?

I started playing for the rangers when I was seventeen and played as a right winger to start with. I then moved into the right side of midfield until I was twenty three. I stopped playing then as I got married and moved to Bedworth. I moved to Coventry a year later and then started back with the Rangers and played sweeper and then full back until they moved into the Midland Combination. I played one more year and in that time I also was player manager of the Reserves.

What other teams did you play for?

I also played for Kenilworth WMC on a Sunday from approx. 1980 until 1983 playing in midfield. In circa 1985 I played on a Sunday with Kenilworth Saints and played as sweeper for them up until I hung my boots up when I was forty two in 2000

Who would you say were the best players that you played with or against?

I have played with some really good players but if I had to name a few in different positions then best players I ever played with were: Goal scorer without a doubt was Paul Barnett, midfielder was Paul (Snowy) Taylor and defender was Keith Bennett.

Are you Tim's cousin?

Yes I am Tim's cousin and in fact he played centre forward for a star charity team against us on one occasion and he was awesome that day at centre forward.

Thanks for your time Bryan.

Kenilworth football in the 1970s

9th January 1971

Five goals for Kenilworth WMC

Jones scored three, one each for Montgomery and O'Malley as Kenilworth WMC beat Wyken WMC 5.0.

22nd April 1971

Carnival mixed football match

Dave Shilton who is Arden Products top scorer will on opposite sides to his wife Shirley. They will play a women's team in aid of the carnival fund.

15th January 1972

A draw for Kenilworth WMC

Jim O'Malley and Colin Dipper scored as Kenilworth WMC drew 2.2 with Leamington St Mary's.

16th September 1972

A good win for first team

Kenilworth WMC beat Wyken Athletic 3.1 with two goals from Barry Jones and a goal from John Clarke.

Five for Kenilworth WMC reserves

Two goals each for Dave Shilton and Steve Beck helped Kenilworth WMC Reserves beat Longford Rangers Reserves 5.0.

2nd October 1976

Stoneleigh score eight goals

Dave Shilton and Peter Sibley were amongst the goals as Stoneleigh beat Newtown Rangers 8.5

3rd April 1976

Kenilworth Rangers are back

After years in the wilderness, Kenilworth Rangers clinched promotion to the Coventry and North Warwickshire Premier Division. A 2.1 win over Coventry Howitzers confirmed promotion the goals were scored by Mike Flay and Paul Barnett. Rangers won a number of trophies between 1947 and 1952; this was the team's first success since them days. Manager Bill Butler and Secretary Dave Sammons built a team for the town to be proud of.

4th October 1978

Thrilling match for Kenilworth

Kenilworth Rangers beat Radford United 8.2, Steve Edgington scored four goals. Kenilworth Rangers squad – Ray Young, Mick Ryan, Barry Reeve, Keith Edgington, Steve Egington, Keith Bennett, Bob Young, John Clarke, Andre Steele, Phil Watkins, Paul Taylor, Robin Burke.

Alan Bryan told me that Steve Edgington was a great finisher; they were striking partners for Racing Club Warwick in the 1980s.

Abbey Rangers

A very successful team in the late 1960s, winning the league in two consecutive seasons and narrowly missing a third in 1970.

11th January 1968

Abbey beat St Bernard's (Sheldon) 2.0 in the Birmingham County Cup thanks to goals from Beaufoy and Samwell.

1st February 1968

Abbey Rangers won 6.0 at Jubilee Athletic in the Coventry and Central Warwickshire Premier League. Alan Smith with three goals the others from Beaufoy and Harvey, the result means that they top the league on goal average.

17th May 1969

Champions retain their crown; Abbey Rangers won the Coventry and Central Warwickshire Premier League by one point. Rangers clinched the title after beating London Road Social 4.2.

Two Ivor Powell's

Barry Powell's father Ivor Powell was a Wales youth international. . Ivor worked at Flavels in Leamington, and was an outside left for Kenilworth Rangers and Warwick Town in the 1950s.

19th December 1952

Hat rick for Ivor

Ivor Powell got a hat rick as Kenilworth Rangers hammered Coventry Road 8.0, Best also scored two and one each for Bostock, Watts and Collett.

13th April 1956

Kenilworth in Cup final

Kenilworth Rangers beat Paget Rangers 1.0 to reach the Birmingham Junior Cup final. Ivor Powell saw a free kick hit the post before J Bostock scored the winning goal.

Kenilworth Rangers – Evans, Knight, Norden, J Bostock, R Bostock, Timiney, Starkey, Watts, Stewart, Powell, Crapp

Kenilworth were unfortunately beaten 1.0 in the final by Smethwick Town which was played at Moor Green in Birmingham. Ivor played in the final and also Routledge who replaced Starkey.

Ivor Powell

The other Ivor was a wing half who played for Queens Park Rangers, Aston Villa and Wales. Ivor managed Bradford City, Port Vale and Carlisle United he was coaching into his nineties entering the Guinness book of records for being the oldest working football coach. In 2004 he was inducted into the Welsh Sports Hall of Fame , he sadly passed away in 2012.

Coventry Plumbing FC

Coventry Plumbing FC currently plays at Gypsy Lane, Kenilworth Town's old ground. Managed by Kev Kingham they currently compete in The Midland League Division Three and are currently second in the table. Coventry Plumbing finished fourth in the 2018/19 season so they are hoping to achieve promotion this season. Kev has previously been manager of Massey Ferguson, Studley, Coventry Copeswood and Kenilworth Town. This season they have thrashed Triumph 9.3 in the Coventry Charity Cup and scored nine again against Coventry Alvis in the Birmingham Saturday Vase.

Football fans in Kenilworth I would encourage you to watch this team as they are going places they want to move up the Midland Football League. Best of luck to Kev and his team.

Kenilworth Wardens

An established club in the town they used to play matches at Leyes Lane but for a number of years they have been based at Glasshouse Lane. Kenilworth Wardens have teams in different age groups and a successful cricket team. The adult team play in the Coventry Alliance Division three and at the time of writing they are fourth in the table.

11th May 2019

Kenilworth Wardens win Benevolent Cup

Wardens beat higher division Bedworth Rangers 4.0 in the cup final at Hawkes Mill, Coventry. Taylor, Jones, Archibald and Pearson with the goals. I watched the highlights on you tube you wouldn't have thought that Wardens were the lower division team. Great finishes from Sam Taylor and Guy Person, well done Wardens.

Engine FC

Engine FC are new to the Tracey Thomas Leamington and District Sunday Football League. Engine FC compete in Division Three and a currently in mid table. The team play at Castle Farm on Fishponds Road in Kenilworth.

Chapter Twelve - Leamington FC 1984 to 1988

I contacted one of Leamington's captains and manager during this period to gather some of their memories.

Ashley Alexander

A combative midfielder Ashley was captain of Leamington in the mid-1980s. I spoke to him on the phone and asked him about his time in football and memories of playing for Leamington.

A Coventry kid Ashley played junior football for Mount Nod Juniors, Woodlands and Holy Family. At the age of fourteen Ashley was playing in men's leagues, he recalls on Saturdays playing for the school in the morning and for a club in the afternoon. As a youngster he played for Coventry Boys and had a trial for Birmingham City. In his late teens he was playing Semi-professional by the end of the 1978/79 he was putting in some strong displays for Racing Club Warwick. Ashley remembers George Anderson, Steve Cooper, Malc Hyland and Paul Coleman from his time with The Racers. In 1983 he missed out on a trip to Wembley with VS Rugby in the FA Vase final, he had a bit of a falling out with Jimmy Knox about being unavailable for some matches. In the early 1980s he played for Bedworth United and Stratford Town as well as playing for top Sunday teams JF Kennedy and Poplar.

In 1985 Ashley joined Leamington FC, at the time the club had been relegated to the Southern League Midland Division. He played a couple of seasons at The Windmill. Ashley told me that the team didn't gel straight away but eventually got some good results. Leamington beat Kidderminster 2.1 in a pre-season game and he got man of the match they weren't happy he remembers!

Ashley spoke highly of Mick Brady and remembers teammates Abbey Kelly, Tony Belcher, Andy Taylor and Ian McConville (Macca) who sadly passed away in 2015.

22nd March 1986

Leamington win vital match

The Brakes beat Oldbury 2.1 With goals from Ashley Alexander and Andy Taylor. Olbury would finish the season bottom of the league one place below Leamington.

Ashley put on the gold shirt of Leamington again in 2004 when a Leamington XI played an All Stars Aston Villa XI which finished 9.0 to Villa!

I asked Ashley via email a couple more questions.

Would you say the Villa players were the best that you played against? Which other players stood out during your career?

The Villa players were up there, but I played against many ex professionals. The best player I played with there were a lot who went on to earn a good living as Professionals but I would say Danny Conway always stands out because it came so easy for him and he had bags of natural skill. I could name so many that I played the likes of Terry Angus, Steve Norris, Ian Crawley, Keith Whiting, Ray Gooding (against him) and Tommy Gorman, to name just a few.

Did you enjoy your time assisting Billy Hollywood at Racing Club Warwick?

The time I was with Billy was good as he was very passionate about the result and we got the best out of the players we had. Considering we didn't have a big budget probably the smallest in the league we did well and created a good tight nick club atmosphere and confidence within. I was there a couple of seasons with Billy.

A couple more Leamington connections, Ashley's son Kane played for Leamington's youth team. Ashley played a season for Newbold Comyn FC.

Since retiring he has achieved Level 1 and 2 FA. Coaching badge UEFA B licence. Management experience with Long Buckby and GPT (Later Coventry Marconi). Ashley was assisted by Abbey Kelly when he managed Coventry Boys they were Wolverhampton Cup Winners. Other coaching and scouting roles with Wolverhampton Wanderers, Leeds United, Birmingham City and Queens Park Rangers.

Late Developers project.(As per Ashley's LinkedIn profile)
Managing my own diary to attend non-league games a month in advance looking for 'late developers' or boys that have been released after their Scholarship/ 1st year pro contract and not been offered a professional contract, with view of inviting for trial with a potential outcome of offering a contract.

Thank you for your time Ashley hopefully see you at a Leamington match.

Paul Smyth

Paul was our last manager before the clubs Abeyance in 1988; I contacted Paul to ask him about his career and time as Leamington manager. Although the summer of 1988 was a sad time for the club and the town we can look back on the 1987/88 season as a time when Paul and his players gave there all for the club and be proud of them. I am sure that Brakes fans are really appreciative of Paul and his player's efforts, indeed everyone else at the club in those days.

Can I firstly ask you how you got into football and what teams you played for?

Like most kids brought up in my era (late 60's and the 70's), I'm 63 now, we always played at school in the playground or when we got home, in the streets, many times right up until the street lights would come on. At that point we'd get a call from Mum to come in!

At Grammar school I played for Warwickshire Schools right up until the age of U16, then after leaving school, at Youth level winning my first Warwickshire County Cap for the U18's, alongside one of my now best friends, Keith Glenn (local Whitnash lad) and one of Coventry City's all-time greats, Trevor Peake. Both Keith and I had our first introduction to "AP Leamington FC" at U19 level, under Manager Ted Forde who was asked (by the now legendary Jimmy Knox) to manage the Youth Team. (I remember Harry Redknapp playing for Leamington at the time.)

During my time playing for Warwickshire Youth, the Manager /Coach was a guy called Alan Perry. A very forward thinking, modern day coach. Some of the style of play I see today by Managers such as Brendan Rogers and Pep Guardiola. Alan was already preaching that style back in the mid-1970s, a Coach way ahead of his time. In the late 70's, after taking a career path which curtailed my playing days, (I had to work weekends) having played for him he asked me if I would like to take up a coaching role? I jumped at the chance .I had some great years coaching, and then Alan got the call from Mick Brady (Leamington Chairman at the time) to help out at Leamington FC Reserves as they were suddenly without a Manager.

Alan agreed to take on the role, but wouldn't commit to doing it long term. This is when he got me involved. He asked me to come along to "help out" After my first game helping Alan, he decided to hand over the reins to me and I took up the role as Player Manager. I was quite successful, on one occasion just missing out on "Manager of the Month" and taking the Reserves from near the bottom of the table to a respectable top half finish by the end of that season.

Before I worked at the weekends, I played for quite a few local teams on Saturdays, but among the more notable ones were Pottertons, Wellesbourne, Woodford United (United Counties League) AP Works, and Kenilworth Rangers (a couple of games I think). But not in that order!

How did getting the Leamington managers job come about?

As I said previously, I was managing the Reserves at Leamington. The first team Manager at the time was John Hanna who was going through a bad run of results with the team at this point. We had a local derby game at "The Windmill" on New Year's Day in January 1987. This was against Coventry Sporting which we lost at which point, straight after the game John tendered his resignation. I was also sitting on the bench that day alongside the rest of the management team as a guest of Johns', representing the Reserves. I went into the clubhouse following the game and one of the directors approached me and asked if I would be interested in helping run the first team. This would be along with another director and well-known local player Keith Orme until at such time they could find a new Manager. At the time the club captain was Steve Thomas, he was also asked to lend a helping hand. Our reign lasted for about three games, at which point they brought in another Leamington legend (from the Graham Allner days), ex Captain, Malcolm Kavanagh.

At the end of the 1986/87 season, the ground was up for sale and the board decided to ditch the First team. They had dropped out of the Southern League and have only one team which would compete in the lower leagues, i.e. the Midland Combination. This then leads to a mass exodus of the existing players I was asked to help out again. But it was a different scenario this time, I was asked to manage the team in the Midland Combination. The only problem I had was I didn't have any players to manage! I needed to work fast before the start of the following season not only trying to put a team together that would do the town proud, but also form a management team. It was at this point I had a stroke of luck. I was working across the road from the ground as a Buyer at AP. The owner of one of my local suppliers was another mad keen local footballer called Stuart Dixon. (Ex Stratford Town).

I asked him if he would be interested in joining me as my Assistant Manager and as luck would have it, he agreed. From that moment onward, I knew with Stuart, he would be dedicated to the cause of retaining local football in the town. This was until at some time in the future, when we lost the ground. I wasn't wrong. There were times when I doubted myself and my abilities, but Stuart kept me going when things always seemed to be stacked against us. He was a good man to have by your side, which I will always be grateful to him for. With Stuart, he also brought a load of local knowledge of players who would not let the club down and would be proud to wear the black and gold colours of Leamington FC. Why local players you might ask? Unlike our predecessors in the Southern League, We had no money to buy players no budget. These guys weren't interested in playing for money they were just proud to play and be involved in their local team.

What are your memories of your time at the club? Do you keep in touch with anyone?

Great memories of people pulling together to try and keep the club going, like Ray Eales our groundsman. Ray along with Mick Brady could be found at many home games, marking out the pitch together and would do anything for the club. The pitch was always a pleasure to play on especially for those local lads who played for me and Stuart; this was hallowed ground for them. Mick Brady who was not only the chairman but a real down to earth guy and true gentleman, also tried to his best to make our time at the club enjoyable. There has been many times since that I've met Mick and he has said to me that those two seasons when I had with the Reserves and the first team, were his most enjoyable. This was due to the fact he wasn't stressed at having to worry about forking out money to players! Another was Keith Hancock, our Match day announcer who lived and breathed Leamington FC. Brian Knibb, who is still there to this day, another Leamington stalwart. All these people had only one thing in mind and that was the survival of their club.

As far as keeping in touch with anyone, apart from my Brother-in-Law Alan Stacey who played for Leamington in the Knox days, and apart from Facebooks I don't really. Since 2009 I've lived near Swansea, but visit Leamington on a regular basis as both my son and daughter and family are still here. On those occasions when I'm walking down the Parade, or out and about at night I'll always bump into someone from those days. People like Steve Montgomery, Arthur Lucey, Willie Fitzpatrick, Vernal Myton. (One of three brothers who played for me that season)

You were quite a young manager did it help having experienced players like Monty, Duncan and Billy J around?

Monty and Dunc couldn't play on a regular basis due to their business commitments, but boy when they did it seemed to lift the whole team especially for the younger less experienced players.

As for "Big" Billy Jawandha who was with me in the reserves and even though living in London, travelled up to Leamington every week to play for "his local" team a true commitment. This type of commitment on and off the pitch was what we tried to install in the squad. Although a lot of the players hadn't played at this level before, people like Mont, Dunc and Billy with their experience certainly lifted the lads on many occasions.

For example when we played Coventry Sporting again at The Windmill in an FA Cup clash in September 1987. Sporting were in the Beazer Homes League (a league above us) and was odds on to win and go through to the next round. Our willingness that day to put everything into the game from the comradery to the never say die attitude. This was coupled with the players like three players previously mentioned constantly cajoling the less experienced, it certainly paid dividends. In front of a capacity crowd, against all the odds we won 2-1. Guess who headed the winner? Yes the big man himself, Billy Jawandha.

With experienced people in mind, you could never forget our Physio, the late great Jack Chapman. His knowledge and experience under Graham Allner was invaluable. Jack would always calm everyone's nerves before each game with his stories. He had a great sense of humour and during the game, his antics on the bench. Priceless! God bless you Jack.

Do you have a favourite match?

My most memorable match would have to be November 1987, against Birmingham City at St Andrews in the Birmingham Senior Cup. We gave a tremendous account of ourselves that night matching the Bluenoses with goals (1-1) right up until the last fifteen minutes. But, due to their superior fitness and experience, we conceded a further three goals by the end of 90 minutes. The full time score was Birmingham City 4.1 Leamington FC. As a club and a bunch of Amateur players, we walked away from the ground that night with our heads held high knowing that we'd given them a game.

My favourite match though was the in the round before the game at St Andrews. It was a midweek game against Sutton Coldfield who was in a league above us. They were also managed by a guy who on my first attempt at my coaching badge back in 1980, was the main coach who gave me a fail! A small point I reminded him about when I went into their Clubhouse after the game.

With a large grin on my face having beaten them by winning 2.1 and breaking my nose in the process whilst playing centre half. (I had to play that night due to the fact that we were down to the bare bones with the amount of players we had signed on).

Towards the end of the season it must have been difficult at times knowing that the club didn't have much time left, you must be very proud of the players and staff at that time?

Planning for another season was impossible. We had to concentrate on what we could control at the time and that was putting a team out each week until we knew the future outcome of the ground. When I looked back at the people I had around me at that time the players, the management team and the directors. Not least the fan base, all wanted the best for the club and I consider it a privilege and an honour to be linked with this great club.

What have you done since Leamington?

Once again my career path meant I had to work weekends. It wasn't until some years later (1998/99 I think) and I was "weekends free" that I had a phone call from Nigel Shanahan. Nigel once of Graham Allners' era and one of the Warwickshire Youth team lads I had the privilege of coaching. He wanted me join him as Assistant Manager over at Southam United. They had just finished runners up in the Midland Combination Premier Division the previous season and had also won the Birmingham Vase. I duly agreed and along with a great young coach at the time called Daryl

White. We had a relatively successful season finishing in third place, but for me that was my final stint in Management.

I eventually finished my involvement in football back in 2003 by teaming up with the lads of Whitnash for a year or two with Danny Walden on Saturdays and Sunday mornings with the Reserves. I was just helping out where I could. At the grand old age of 50 I turned out one morning and played 90 minutes when the Reserves were short of players.

Thank you very much for your time Paul.

Chapter Thirteen - Family Connections

Footballing families with connections to the towns of Leamington, Warwick or Kenilworth.

Mancini

In the late 1970s and early 1980s four brothers were playing football at a good level in Leamington and Warwick. Steve and Cliff Mancini were strikers, Alan and Paul defenders. Their father Cliff Mancini snr played for Saltisford Rovers in the 1950s with his brother Ernie Mancini.

Steve Mancini

I spoke to Steve on the phone and asked him a few questions about his career. Steve played most notably for Avana Sports, Avon Rovers and Pottertons. One memorable match he scored six goals v Wellesbourne Youth, Steve recalls one game he lobbed Eric Overton from forty yards!

Steve and Cliff were both prolific goal scorers often very close who scored the most goals. Steve talked about some of the great players back in the day, he said Mick Mackey was a superb midfielder (Mick is Ben Mackey's dad) Johnny Woodhouse had a wand of a left foot, Robin Hood and Paul Cooke were also great players.

Steve and Mick Williams started Saturday football at Radford Semele FC; they were there ten years and ended up with two teams and a few trophies.

Steve's son Jack is also a decent player he is currently manager of Hampton Magna FC, a bit more about Jack in another chapter. At the age of 61 Steve is still scoring goals in walking football which is played at the Oval in Bedworth.

It was great speaking to Steve; he feels that these days there are a lot of distractions for players in today's world. In his day there wasn't any X boxes or any I pads, every bit of spare time they were out playing football.

Mancini in the news

12th May 1950

Saltisford Rovers loose at Villa Park

Saltisford lost 3.2 against Bromford Amateurs in the final of the Aston Villa Cup, Gwynne scored both of Rovers goals. Cliff and Ernie Mancini both had good games and were unlucky to be on the losing side.

Saltisford Rovers – R Hunt, Stradling, Haines, Manley, E Hunt, E Mancini, J Hunt, Flaherty, Walker, Gwynne, C Mancini

18th April 1952

Saltisford beat Lockheed 5.0

An impressive win over neighbours Lockheed, Ernie and Cliff Mancini contributed to a fine win. Montgomery with two goals, two own goals and a goal from Stradling.

22nd January 1954

Champions beaten by Saltisford Rovers

South Warwickshire League Champions Cheltenham Town Reserves were beaten 5.3 by Saltisford. King, Combstock, Mancini and Gwynne amongst the goals for the Warwick side.

29th October 1977

Double hat rick for Steve

Steve Mancini scored six goals as Avon Rovers hammered Wellesbourne Youth Club 11.1. Cliff Mancini scored two goals, Kevin Doyle and Roger Clarke completed the scoring.

21st January 1978

Mancini brothers score in rout

Avon Rovers beat Offchurch Sports 9.0, Steve Mancini scored three goals. Alan and Cliff Mancini with two goals each, Neil Benton and Allan Dyer completed the scoring.

28th January 1978

Cliff Mancini equals individual goal scoring record

Avon Rovers hammered Wellesbourne Youth Club 13.0; Cliff Mancini got eight of the goals. Steve Mancini with two, Tommy Aitken, Roger Clarke and Neil Benton with a goal each.

25th March 1978

Avana Sports put nine past Mid Warwickshire Police

Robin Hood and Cliff Mancini both got hat tricks and a brace from Steve Mancini

20th October 1979

Avon Rovers hit ten goals

Cliff Mancini scored two goals, Paul and Steve Mancini both scored. Phil Haycock, Roger Clarke, Binder Braich and Kevin Dyer also scored.

Kelly

Leamington fans will be familiar with Errington Kelly and Abbey Kelly who both played for The Brakes in the 1980s. Errington was with AP Leamington in 1981 his younger brother Abbey played for Leamington in the 1985/86 season. Tony Kelly had a good career in professional football, brothers Mel and Charlie also played at a good standard of Non-league football. Let's now have a look at this fine footballing family from Coventry.

Abbey Kelly

Tony and Mel's older brother Abbey was a good midfielder, I had the pleasure of speaking to him on the phone. Abbey and the rest of the family lived in Tile Hill Lane by the Standard Triumph factory and the brothers went to Woodlands School. As a youngster Abbey played for Mount Nod Juniors, before he left school he signed forms for Coventry City. The talented youngster just missed out on an apprenticeship, in his age group there was Ian Muir and Peter Hormantschuk, only Peter made it through to the first team at Highfield Road. Abbey played for a number of local non – league sides including Triumph Athletic, Coleshill , Bedworth, Coventry Sporting , St Albans City (with Tony for a short period) and Stratford Town(Under Stuart Dixon).

In the 1985/86 season Abbey played for Leamington FC, at that time The Brakes had just been relegated to the Southern League Midland Division. It wasn't a great time for the club as they struggled at the bottom of the table. Abbey's older brother Errington had played for the club earlier in the decade however a lot had changed at the club since then. Abbey played alongside Ashley Alexander at The Old Windmill they were friends since playing for Coventry School Boys. The Brakes managers were John Williams then John Hanna

5th October 1985

Leamington earn fine away win

Abbey scored as Leamington beat Gloucester City 3.2 away, Steve Johnson and Bob McKay also scored.

Abbey later played for Racing Club Warwick; in The Beazer Homes Midland Division in 1991 they had a strong squad of players.

Goalkeepers – Andy Russell, Shaun Hemming

Defenders – Alec Brotherton ,Len Derby, Martin Lander, Mark Titterton, Richard Holt, Adrian Passey

Midfield – Abbey Kelly, Gary Hannam, Martin Smith, Darrell White, Keith Mardenborough, Adrian Fitzhugh

Forwards – Darren Deeley, Jamie Wootton, Kevin Watts, Tommy Hathaway

Abbey and Len(Derby) are still good friends, they played at Coventry Sporting together too. Thank you for your help Abbey great to speak to you.

Tony Kelly

I had the pleasure of contacting Nyrere Anthony Okpara "Tony" Kelly via email. Tony and his twin brother Omele (Mel) were born in Coventry on 14th February 1966. I asked Tony about his football career and memories.

Could you tell me how you and Mel got into football?

Myself Nyrere (I use my middle name Anthony since I was eighteen) and Omele (Mel) loved our childhood playing days. Our first club was Coundon Cockerills under 10's, and then we both went on to play for Mount Nod, whilst still playing for Woodlands from Under 12 to Under 16. My most memorable game was a Woodlands Cup Final v Bishop Ullathorne where we won 2.0 and I scored both. It was on back of Coventry Evening Telegraph and I couldn't wait to get to paper shop to read the report!

After my school years I joined Abbey at Stratford Town after being released by Bristol City aged seventeen. Mel and I signed for Bristol City at sixteen on the YTS scheme. Ex Leeds legend Terry Cooper gave us a chance, and I became the youngest player to play for Bristol City first team at 16-244 days!

We had a great time in Bristol but my wild living caught up with me. Mel was released first, and then five months later I was released even though I had played six times in first team. I don't think bringing girls back to the lodgings at 2am helped our cause!

Mel played for – Billericay, Enfield town, Berkhampstead, Dulwich Hamlet and Corinthians Casuals

Errington was a great player; you must have looked up to him?

Errington was at Bristol rovers at the time and he was a fantastic player, we looked up to him. Errington obviously went on to play for Lincoln Bristol City and Peterborough. It still wrangles with the family that Errington, although top scorer in the Coventry City reserves Central League, Bobby Gould never gave him his First Division debut! Errington was more than good enough to play in the First Division at the time. Abbey was also released from Coventry at sixteen, and never got an apprenticeship, again a joke!!!

Can you tell me about your later career?

So when Errington moved to Sweden at twenty nine it was left for me to pick up the mantle! I moved to London with Mel at eighteen. I played for Dulwich Hamlet, Cheshunt, Enfield Town - and finally St Albans City. Whilst at St Albans as a twenty year old I got an offer to play in Sweden's Second Division with Gimonas CK.

It was a great experience in Sweden and I became a better player. It was only a one season contract, so when I returned to St Albans all the scouts were watching me. Trials at Watford and Southampton followed before Stoke City and Alan Ball (World Cup legend) signed me for £40.000. So I got my second chance at twenty two, I then Played at Championship level.

One story - I was playing at the Hawthorns against West Bromwich, and it was a wet cold Tuesday night. I went up for a header and felt a bang in my jaw! My teeth were knocked out- it was agony! My two teeth are still screwed in today and who done it? Craig Shakespeare! !!! Mr Leicester City lol

What were your best and worst moments as a professional?

Best game as a pro:

Has to be that night at Anfield I scored an 89th minute equaliser through Grobbelaar's legs!! Stoke City fans still message me on social media today about it.

Worst moment:

The return leg v Liverpool, a 29.000 sell out at the Victoria ground. I gave a back pass to Ian rush! We lost 2.3.!! Jimmy Greaves said on TV - what was he thinking!

Second best moment

Winning the Autoglass Trophy at Wembley in 1991. Mark Stein got the winning goal in front of 65.000 fans. My Family were there for that memorable day.

I went on to play for - Bury fc, Cardiff City loan, Hull City loan, Colchester United loan, Leyton Orient and Falkirk loan. I played approximately 200 league games.

I fell into gambling addiction during my nine year career. I lost over £500.000 including my house. Eight years ago I sought help and got counselling and family support. I decided to put my story to print in 2014 with my book Red Card. Feedback was fantastic and I done lots of media work which made me realise I must do more. So I set up my company Red Card gambling support project. I now facilitate and educate young people on the dangers if gambling. I have been endorsed by parliament and done talks as far as Dohar! I will continue to educate and make a difference.

The rest of the family are Charlie Kelly (Triumph Athletic) Ian Kelly (no football- army service) and one sister-Patricia Kelly bless her.

We thought highly of the following players as 15/16 year olds: which we all played at the same time, a great era. - Mark Rosegreen, Terry Angus, Mick Shearer, Pete Shearer, Andy Williams, Mark Mercury, John Mathews, Gareth Evans, Lloyd Wilcox, Dean Riley and Tim Flowers.

Memorable match

Stoke City 1.0 Stockport County - Autoglass Trophy final, 16th May 1992

Tony talked about winning the Autoglass Trophy (Associate Members Cup) at Wembley. Stoke City were in the Third Division under Lou Macari they would win promotion the following year. The trophy win at Wembley brought welcome cheer to Stoke fans it would be the beginning of the clubs revival. Mark Stein scored the winning goal, like Tony he came from a good footballing family.

Stoke City –
Fox,Butler,Kevan,Cranson,Overson,Sandford,Kelly,Foley,Biggins,Stein,Heath

Thank you for sharing your memories with me Tony, I look forward to reading your book. You are an inspiration what you have been through and come out the other side to help others. We are all proud of you.

Red Card is available on Amazon, Tony's website is
Kellysredcardconsultancy.co.uk

Errington Kelly

Errington Edison Kelly was born on 8th April 1958 in Saint Vincent but moved to Coventry when he was a kid. A fast player who often played on the wing but preferred playing up front as a striker. Errington is known best for his time with Peterborough averaging one goal in four.

In the late 1970s he was one of the best players in Coventry football and he was destined to play at a higher level. In 1980 Errington joined AP Leamington he played ten games in all competitions scoring three goals but his first team chances were limited due to Duncan Gardner and Doug Hickton being first choice strikers. Errington's best game for AP was as a super sub scoring twice against Maidstone in September 1980. He had spells with VS Rugby and Ledbury Town before being spotted by Division Three team Bristol Rovers. At that time Bristol Rovers had a few well known players such as Gary Mabbutt, Keith Curle, Ian Holloway, Alan Ball and Mick Channon. The Pirates manager was Bobby Gould who would become Coventry City manager in 1983. Errington also played for Bristol City and Lincoln City before joining The Sky Blues in the summer of 1983. Teammates at Rovers Graham Withey and Nicky Platnauer would also join Bobby Gould's team. Coventry City had a major change of players this summer Bobby used his knowledge of the lower leagues to sign players like Stuart Pearce and also added the experienced Sam Allardyce to his defence. Former England striker Charlie George played in pre-season but didn't sign permanently. Errington despite scoring on a regular basis for the reserves never played for the first team. Bobby liked to play a big man small man combination, unfortunately for Errington Terry Gibson was first choice. Terry was paired with Dave Bamber or Graham Withey at the end of the season Mick Ferguson joined on loan. Errington joined Peterborough United on loan then signed for The Posh permanently he played the best football of his career at London Road. In the late 1980s he spent a season in Sweden, since retiring from playing Errington has been an English teacher in Coventry and Birmingham. There is a good interview with Errington on you tube he talked about his career. It is a shame that he never played for Coventry's first team he was certainly good enough, however he can be proud of his career a great player in this fine footballing family.

Errington in the news

28th October 1972

Hat rick for Errington

Woodlands under -15 beat Sydney Stringer 7.1 with Errington scoring three. Tom Kelly (no relation) also scored three goals, Lawrence Coleman completed the scoring. Ricky Carter scored Sidney Stringers consolation goal.

24th November 1979

Triumph win at Sphinx

Errington scored a first half goal as Triumph won 2.0 at Coventry Sphinx.

Leon Kelly

Nephew / cousin of the Kelly brothers, Leon played in the Football League for Cambridge United. I contacted Leon on Facebook and asked him a few questions about his football career. Leon is well known to football fans in

Warwickshire he has played for several midland clubs including a spell with Stratford Town in 2009.

When you were growing up it must have been cool your uncles being footballers, did they inspire you to become one yourself?

Yes my cousin Tony Kelly was at Stoke City at the time playing under Lou Macari.
He did inspire me and also I liked Tony Daley at Aston Villa because we had similar hair and he was quick like me. I was supposed to sign for Stoke at sixteen but the life of a young boy with friends and girls distracted me lol

What club did you enjoy the most?

The club I enjoyed most was Worcester City really if I had to pick one. But Hinckley United was just as good, great memories

I remember seeing you play in the FA cup on the TV for Worcester it must have been a great experience?

.

Yes it was the second round of the FA cup against Huddersfield we lost 1-0 then we heard the news in the changing rooms that they had drawn Chelsea away in the third round
It was also great as Mark Bright commented saying I was like a Thierry Henry lol and that I just had my second child four weeks ago

Your second match for Cambridge you came up against Neil Ruddock do you remember that match ?

Yes Razor Ruddock away at Swindon absolutely smashed me into the side board's lol As if to say welcome to the professional game. I remember getting up off the floor mud all down me and white paint all down one side ha-ha…

Were you ever at Coventry city in your junior career?

I was at Coventry Boys, Warwickshire County U14s and went to Coventry Academy. I mainly had trials at Notts County and Derby County before nearly signing for Stoke City. I was at St Thomas More School where I started at the age of ten playing for U12s Then played at Mount Nod from then on until age of sixteen.

My hero's growing up were big Cyrille Regis and Dave Bennett, I had the pleasure to play at Atherstone United with Benno. Lloyd McGrath is like family his cousin married my cousin we act like we're family for years now.

Thanks Leon for sharing your memories with me

Leon in the news

8th September 2009

Leon at the double for Stratford Town

Leon scored two goals on his debut for Stratford in a 2.0 win away at Loughborough University in The Midland Alliance.

24th April 2013

Coventry Alvis win Coventry Charity Cup

Leon helped Alvis beat Bolehall Swifts 2.0 at the Ricoh Arena; Alvis included former Coventry City and Cameroon striker Patrick Suffo. Christian Jordan and Steve Evans scored Alvis's goals.

Many thanks for your time Leon.

I meet up with Ken Brown often for a cup of tea, Ken remembers the Kelly brothers when he was manager of Triumph Athletic and spoke highly of them. It has been a pleasure including the Kelly family and making contact with Abbey, Tony and Leon.

Camkin

Bill Camkin

A Leamington resident who was an important figure in the history of snooker and Birmingham City FC.

Born in London in 1894 Bill came to prominence in the 1920s through his involvement in various aspects of billiards and snooker. Bill ran a billiards hall called Camkin's Hall in Birmingham which hosted the early days of the World snooker Championships including the 1927 and 1928 finals. Bill was the referee for the 1927 final when the legendary Joe Davis beat Tom Dennis by sixteen frames to seven. Joe Davis dominated snooker for three decades.

In 1939 Bill was made honorary managing-director of Birmingham FC, he took over secretarial duties and shared team management until 1944. Bill remained on the board at St Andrews until ill health in 1951. He is highly regarded at the club; Bill helped keep the club going during the war and was bought a commemorative cigarette box which was bought by Birmingham players and staff. St Andrews was bombed in January 1942 which destroyed the main stand.

Bill along with Dave Montgomery and a local Police Inspector set up Leamington Boys club in Gloucester Street. Bill took youngsters Dave and Ted (Tich) Eden for trials at Birmingham FC, both Dave and Ted played for Lockheed Leamington. Dave played for The Blues Reserves and made one appearance for the first team during the war years.

Bill owned the Spa Hotel in Holly Walk, Leamington the family home. At the age of sixty one he sadly passed away at home on the 26th April 1956.

John Camkin

A Leamington resident son of Bill Camkin, John was a journalist, football, business and sports administrator. Well known locally for his travel company and being a director at Coventry City Football Club. John was born in Kings Norton in Worcestershire on 23rd June 1922, he attended

Warwick School. In the second world war John served in the Royal Air Force, after the war he resumed his career in journalism. John worked as a sports writer for the Birmingham Gazette and commentated for BBC radio covering the 1954, 1958, and 1962 World Cups. In 1966 he was part of the ITV team which covered the 1966 World Cup in England. John also wrote several books including the Play fair Football Annual and a book about the 1958 World Cup.

John became known in Leamington Spa when he bought a travel agency and opened a few shops in the area known as John Camkin Travel Ltd. In 1972 he sold his business to the Thomson Holidays Travel Group and his travel shops were re-branded Lunn Poly.

John became director of Coventry City in 1962 and was instrumental in bringing Jimmy Hill to the club. The Sky Blue Song to the tune of 'the Eton Boating Song' was written by Jimmy and John. Jimmy Hill transformed the clubs fortunes and The Sky Blues won the Second Division in 1967 winning promotion to the top flight of English football for the first time in their history.

In May 1972 Coventry City won the Camkin Cup beating Tamworth 3.2 over two legs. Brian Joicey had given Sky Blues a two goal first leg lead. In the second leg at Highfield Road, Tamworth won 2.1 on the night with goals from Millard and Jessop. Alan Dugdale scored Coventry City's goal.

In 1976 John along with Jimmy Hill and Leamington man Olaf Dixon went to Saudi Arabia with World Sports Academy to develop football. Jimmy and John ventured into North America with Detroit Express it turned out to be unsuccessful and Jimmy lost a lot of money. Detroit Express was part of the now defunct North American Soccer League, a few well known players played for them – Trevor Francis, Alan Brazil, Ted McDougall, David Bradford and Gary Bannister.

John also ran The Secretaries' and Managers' Association, Olaf Dixon has recently been made vice president of the association. In the 1980s John managed golfers Howard Clark and Pip Elson who is from Leamington. In the 1990s he was chairman of Leamington Tennis Court Club, John lived in Lansdowne Circus in the town he sadly passed away on the 19th June 1998 aged 75.

Both Bill and John contributed greatly to sport in this country, we should be proud that they were residents of Royal Leamington Spa.

Crawley

A family name that doesn't stand out straight away in regards to connections with Leamington, Warwick or Kenilworth. However the third generation of this family gave a Leamington legend his finest hour as a manager.

Tommy Crawley (Senior)

A centre forward who began his career with his local team Blantyre Victoria then Hamilton Academicals. In 1934 Tommy signed for Motherwell playing eight times and scoring nine goals including three against Cowdenbeath. In 1935 he joined Preston North End teaming up with Bill Shankly but only played a couple of games for the club. In February 1936 Tommy joined Coventry City as cover for Clarrie Bourton, he began to establish himself in the 1938/39 season scoring fourteen times from eighteen league appearances. During the war years Tommy also guested for Nottingham Forest, he retired in 1948. A few Leamington connections from his time at Highfield Road include Dennis Tooze and Eric Dobbs (Lockheed Leamington) Ted Roberts (Flavels) and Les Bruton (Leamington Town). Tommy scored an impressive eight goals against West Bromwich Albion in the war years, he sadly passed away in 1977.

Tommy Crawley (Junior)

A striker for Bedworth Town, Corby, Worcester City and Hinckley Athletic. Tommy is best remembered for his time at Nuneaton Borough. In the 1966/67 season Boro reached the third round of the FA Cup famously beating a Swansea team who included Ivor Allchurch 2.0 in the second round. Tommy scored in that match against Swansea, he also helped Boro finish second in the Southern League Premier Division the same season. Tommy sadly passed away in September 2015.

Ian Crawley

Born in Coventry in May 1962, Tommy's son Ian went to Bishop Ullathorne School in the city. The talented youngster played for Coventry Schools, Mount Nod and Europa before joining Coventry Sphinx aged sixteen. In 1977 Ian followed his dad's footsteps in signing for Nuneaton Borough, when Ian first broke into the team at Manor Park he asked fans not to compare him to his dad and to judge him on his own performances. In the late 1970s Nuneaton Borough had some talented players in Trevor Peake, Brian Alderson and future AP Leamington centre forward Cliff Campbell.

Ian is best remembered for his time with VS Rugby under former AP Leamington manager Jimmy Knox.

On the 30th April 1983 Ian scored the winning goal for VS Rugby as they beat Halesowen Town 1.0 in the FA Vase Final. A legend at Butlin Road Ian scored 122 for the club. In 1989 Ian scored the winning goal at Wembley again this time for Telford United in the FA Trophy final. Ian also played for Bedworth United, Tamworth, Kettering Town and Solihull Borough. Ian sadly passed away in Myton Hospice in 2008 aged 49 after a long battle with motor neurone disease.

Three generations of great strikers, certainly a Warwickshire family to be proud of.

McKinley

Tim McKinley

I contacted Tim McKinley via email, Tim is the second generation of this fine footballing family. The McKinley family have three generations of footballers and a long association with Fords Sports which used to be called Imperial Sports .John McKinley (Tim's father) played for Warwick Town in the late 1940s.

Who did your dad (John McKinley) play for in his playing days and how long was he a manager?

My dad played for Bishop Auckland and Hartlepool Town before the war but enlisted in the navy in1939 at twenty two for the duration of the war .After the war he moved to Leamington with my mum to work at Fords. According to my much older brother he played for Fords for several years, he then went on to manage them for about fifteen years till about 1977.At one time he was told he had to many players who didn't work there and he had to put more players that worked at Fords so he packed it in and came to watch me play and help out with that team.

What teams did you play for?

I started playing for a pub team called the Jack and Jill when I was fifteen in the fourth Division of the Sunday League. Our goalkeeper was' Banger' Walsh the local wrestling celebrity. They changed their name to Lillington Sports a year later and went from the fourth Division to the then Premier in successive years .I then went to play for long Itchington for the next ten years on Saturday's. I also played for leam Hibs Southam United, Racing Club Warwick, Kenilworth Town and a short spell when I was 17/18 at wolves in their reserves on a two year non-contract but it didn't work out.

Did you know that the Leamington Sunday league won the W H Harrison shield four out of five years which was contested between all the Sunday leagues in the Birmingham County FA in the early 1980s. I'm surprised that I've never seen it mentioned. Also my son has played for Westlea for the last thirteen years so between my brother Steve, me and my son we have won the Leamington Sunday First Division title approximately 22/23 times.

What teams did your brothers play for and what positions did they play?

Steve and Chris my older brothers both played for Fords Steve went on to play for the Jet and Whittle and long Itchington. Chris played for Leamington Celtic; they both played for Pottertons and AP Works teams on a Saturday. Steve moved to Bournemouth in1981 and played in the Bournemouth Premier League until he was forty nine although he did go from no nine to sweeper at the end. Chris was a dodgy full back which when were together always joke about much to his annoyance.

Do you remember any other players when you were at Wolves?

Being a Leeds supporter the main one I remember was Wayne Clarke brother of Alan' Sniffer' Clarke from the great Leeds team of the 1960s and 1970s. Phil Parkes the goalie mainly because he was very vocal in the dressing room at half time if we were losing .It was scary for a eighteen year old from Leamington used to keep my head down and hope he didn't shout at me

Andy McKinley

Andy progressed through the youth team at Leamington and made three appearances for the first team. In February 2004 he made his Brakes debut against Alveston in the Midland Combination Premier Division. A centre half that spent time with Coventry City's academy with Ben Mackey. Tim mentioned he played for Westlea Wanderers, Andy also played for Whitnash Town and was part of the squad that won the 2014 Coventry Charity Cup.

McKinley in the news

27th October 1951

Imperial Sports score seven goals

Imperial Sports beat Coventry Amateur Reserves 7.2 at Myton Road. Bugg scored four goals, McKinley, Waterhouse and Talbot also scored. Cooper scored twice for Amateurs, they were no match for the home team with Bugg and McKinley impressive.

19th October 1956

Two penalties in cup win

McKinley scored two penalties as Imperial Sports beat Rootes 4.3 in the Rugby Chamber of Commerce Cup. Wootton and Burns also scored for the Leamington side.

30th November 1956

Imperial Sports earn draw

Imperial drew 2.2 with Daimler at Coventry; they played most of the second half with ten men because of an injury to left back Whitmore. McKinley and Raven scored for Sports.

18th March 1978

Lillington Sports force extra time

Lillington Sports from Division Four forced Division One team B&B Trailers to extra time in the Leamington League Challenge Cup. They eventually lost 4.2 with Jim O'Malley and Steve Edgington with two each for B&B Trailers. Tim McKinley and Frank Daly scored for Lillington Sports.

8th December 1979

Entertaining draw

Long Itchington and Avon Star drew 2.2 , Steve McKinley and Bobby Hancock's for Long Itchington. Neil Thompson with a brace for Avon Star

30th September 1972

Whittle Wanderers win at Leamington Southend

Olly Guinane got a hat rick, Steve McKinley also scored for Whittle. Alan Bryan and John Caden replied for Southend.

18th February 1978

Premier Division leaders score ten

Long Itchington hammered Radford United 10.2 with Bobby Hancock's scoring four of them. Steve McKinley, Mick Palis and John Woodhouse scored two goals each. Neil Mucklow netted both for Radford.

3rd March 1979

Tim McKinley hat-rick

Tim scored three goals as Leamington Hibernians as they thrashed Kenilworth Rangers by nine goals.

Thank you very much for your time Tim.

Dougall

Jimmy Dougall

A tricky winger who joined Coventry City in the 1919/20 season, Jimmy began his career with Clelland Juniors and Motherwell. Jimmy made 237 appearances for Coventry City scoring 14 goals. During his time at Highfield Road he played with England international Danny Shea and fellow Scot George Chaplin.

In 1924 he was the subject of a £2,000 transfer bid from Manchester United but Coventry City turned it down. Jimmy joined Reading in 1926 for £555 but after twelve games for the Royals he broke his leg badly which forced his retirement. Jimmy would have been twenty six and in his prime, I am certain that he would have gone on to achieve a lot in the game. The first great Scottish player to play for Coventry City possibly the best player for the club in the 1920s. After retiring from football he returned to Coventry to work for Morris Motors. Jimmy had six sons, Jimmy junior had brief spell on Coventry City's books. Jimmy sadly passed away in November 1966.

Gordon Dougall

Jimmy's son Gordon was a talented player and later became a successful manager.

In October 1952 Gordon was aged seventeen and playing for Morris Motors in Coventry. The young inside right signed professional forms for Derby County. In October 1955 Gordon joined Bedworth Town he was a regular in Derby County's Central League team for three years. Twenty one year old Gordon lived locally in Swan Lane, Coventry. In 1956 Gordon joined Lockheed Leamington under manager Les Latham.

Gordon joined Atherstone in October 1961 at the same time as Lockheed teammate David Newey. Lockheed had a very strong squad of players back then, Syd Hall and Ernie Ward were establishing themselves as first choice wide players.

In December 1968 Gordon was appointed new manager of West Midland League team Bedworth United. Gordon brought in Bill Mooney and George Awde as his assistants, George also previously played for Lockheed Leamington. Gordon had previously been player-manager of Atherstone for three years. Gordon was also manager of Tamworth in the 1970s. Sadly Gordon passed away in December 2019; Ken Brown called me to tell me the sad news. Ken was a long-time friend of Gordon and George Awde who passed away in 2004.

Tommy Dougall

Gordon's elder brother like his father Jimmy he was a right winger. Tommy played for Morris Motors, Coventry City, Guildford City (loan),

Brentford, Sunderland and Yeovil Town. During the 1948/49 season he played three times for Sunderland teammates included England internationals Len Shackleton and Ivor Broadis. Tommy was manager of Hillingdon Borough and Kingstonian in the 1960s. He sadly passed away in January 1997 aged seventy five.

Final thoughts

I hope that you have enjoyed this trip down football memory lane and have enjoyed reading it as much as I have liked writing it. I have tried to include as many local teams and players as possible I apologise if I have missed anyone out.

This book wouldn't have been possible without the help everyone has given me, thank you so much everyone.

Acknowledgements

I would like to thank the following people who have helped me with this book; your time is very much appreciated. If I have missed anyone I do apologise.

Vikram Singh (For use of your lovely photo of Chesterton Windmill),Tom Lewin, Dave Garratt, Alan Bryan, Keith Gould, Pep Gill, Don Grantham, Mark Davison, Chris Walker, Chris Prophet, Steve Hopcroft, Jamie Coleman, Nick McFarlane, Paddy Crowley, Carl Goddard, Dudley Roberts, Gordon Simms, Mandy Thorneywork, Ken Lambert, Nigel Croft, Tom Cooper, Eric Canning, Ian Montgomery, Chris Pheasey, Jodie Wildman, Alan Vest, Claudio Cardellino, Steve Mancini, Jack Mancini, Ian Shurvinton, Kelvin Evans, Gill George, Lance Clarke, Alan Guilford, Mick Murphy, Malcolm Jukes, Eddy Kostiuk, Roger Talbot, Duncan Gardner, Ajit Braich, Ken Probin, Mark Rowlatt, Rebecca Clarke, Ian King, Alexander Camkin, Mike Berry, Dennis Farr, Ian Billington, Dave Sharpe, Rob Dent, Dave Draper, Steve Fox, Micky Fox, Wendy Morby, Pauline Farrell, Pete Roper, Darren Deeley, Roy Russell, Brian Knibb, Ian Bettles , Graham Timms, Alan Stacey, Chris Coleman, Marcus Hamill, Paul Smyth , Steve Montgomery, Lisa and Simon Rea, Roger Bain, Len Derby, Barry Powell, Glen Webb, Tony Kelly, Leon Kelly, Abbey Kelly, Stuart Hepburn, David Vicary, Ashley Alexander, Jet Kang, Nev Hawtin, Donna Barnett, Mick Burke, Sean Burke, Gurpreet Dosanjh, Dennis Woodhead, Gerry Gleeson, Geoff Bott, Roy Slade, Darren Slater, Bob Phillips, Keith Hancock, Bryan Flowers, Ray Bethell, Ian Cosgrove , Ian Goodwin. Jamie Wootton, Steve Sykes, Siobhàn Gordon, Jim Barry, Jim Brown, Paul Vanes and Leamington Football Club.

Printed in Great Britain
by Amazon